THE BEST
Convection
Oven COOKBOOK

THE BEST
Convection
Oven COOKBOOK

Linda Stephen

Robert ROSE

For complete cataloguing information, see page 184.

Disclaimer
The recipes in this book have been carefully tested by our kitchen and our tasters. To the best of our knowledge, they are safe and nutritious for ordinary use and users. For those people with food or other allergies, or who have special food requirements or health issues, please read the suggested contents of each recipe carefully and determine whether or not they may create a problem for you. All recipes are used at the risk of the consumer. Consumers should consult their convection oven manufacturer's manual for recommended procedures and cooking times.

We cannot be responsible for any hazards, loss or damage that may occur as a result of any recipe use.

For those with special needs, allergies, requirements or health problems, in the event of any doubt, please contact your medical advisor prior to the use of any recipe.

Design & Production: PageWave Graphics Inc.
Photography: Mark T. Shapiro
Editorial: Shelley Tanaka
Food Styling: Kate Bush
Prop Styling: Charlene Erricson
Color Scans & Film: Colour Technologies

Cover image: Roast Chicken with Orange and Sage (page 173)

The publisher and author wish to express their appreciation to the following suppliers of props used in the food photography:

DISHES, LINENS AND ACCESSORIES

Homefront
371 Eglinton Ave. W.
Toronto, Ontario M5N 1A3
Tel: (416) 488-3189
www.homefrontshop.com

FLATWARE

Gourmet Settings Inc.
245 West Beaver Creek Rd., Unit 10
Richmond Hill, Ontario L4B 1L1
Tel: 1-800-551-2649
www.gourmetsettings.com

We acknowledge the financial support of the Government of Canada through the Book Publishing Industry Development Program (BPIDP) for our publishing activities.

Published by Robert Rose Inc.
120 Eglinton Ave. E., Suite 1000, Toronto, Ontario, Canada M4P 1E2
Tel: (416) 322-6552; Fax: (416) 322-6936

Printed in Canada

1 2 3 4 5 6 7 8 9 10 GP 11 10 09 08 07 06 05 04 03

TO THE MEMORY of my father, George Stephen
(who would say when I was a young experimenting cook
that every dish tasted fine, even while he was adding another
spoonful of chili sauce!), and to my mother, Doris Stephen,
for years of cheerfulness and practical suggestions and
teaching me to make angel cake. She still eats my food but
will whip up a wonderful ("Nothing fancy!") salmon loaf
or pudding on days when I can't cook another thing.

Contents

Acknowledgments 9

Introduction 11

    About Convection Cooking 12

        Oven Settings 12

            Convection Bake 12

            Convection Roast 13

            Convection Broil 14

        Converting and Adapting Recipes 14

        Cookware and Containers 15

        General Tips 16

        Food Safety 16

        About These Recipes 17

        Convection Toaster Ovens 17

Appetizers and Soups 19

Fish and Seafood 33

Poultry 45

Meat 61

One-Dish Suppers 81

Vegetables and Salads 95

Breakfast, Brunch and Lunch 113

Quickbreads and Cookies 127

Desserts 145

Convection Toaster Oven 163

Index 185

Acknowledgments

MANY FRIENDS AND PROFESSIONALS HELPED TO BRING THIS book together. Special thanks go to the following:

- Convection oven experts Alex Brown of Integrated Appliances Ltd. for the use of the DCS wall unit ovens, Beverly Melnick of Cuisinart Canada for the use of the convection toaster oven; Graydon McIntosh, McIntosh General Store, Coldsprings; Jeron Ashitei of Electrolux Home Products.

- Bob Dees and the team at Robert Rose Inc. — Andrew Smith, Joseph Gisini, Kevin Cockburn and Daniella Zanchetta at PageWave Graphics; Mark Shapiro and Charlene Erricson; Jennifer MacKenzie and Teresa Makarewicz.

- Bonnie Stern, for many years of friendship and cooking camaraderie, and for recommending me for this project.

- Kim Pedersen, for her hours of typing and retyping and her computer skills.

- Jackie Berdar, Rhonda Caplan, Shirley Dearle, Liz Knowles, Maureen Lollar and Josée Ménard, for their recipe testing, good humor, tasting skills and recipe and ingredient expertise.

- Kate Bush, for her outstanding and stylish ways with food presentation.

- Shelley Tanaka, editor extraordinaire, who untangled my sentences and thoughts to say what I really meant.

- Students and friends who make the trek to the country for cooking classes. Thanks always for the suggestions, smiles and "homework" reports.

- Bill Vronsky, an avid food taster and special friend who provided encouragement and technical and electrical assistance.

- My family — Clarke, Susan, Harry, Kathy, Craig, Jennifer, Jenna and Chad — for their tasting and retasting and for participating in impromptu meals, whether it was all vegetables one day and all desserts the next.

Introduction

CONVECTION OVENS HAVE BEEN USED FOR YEARS IN HOTEL and restaurant kitchens, bakeries and pizza parlors. These ovens have now been adapted for the home kitchen. There are models suitable for large or small kitchens, and they come with a dizzying variety of features and combinations. You may have acquired one in your new place.

Although sales of convection ovens and toaster ovens increase annually, there are few cookbooks available for convection oven cooking. As a result, many new owners are intimidated by the convection option, so they continue to rely on the standard oven features, ignoring the advantages of convection cooking.

But this oven is not a monster; it is safe, economical, convenient and easy to use.

In my years of catering, baking, teaching and working in the food industry, I have used the convection oven for various tasks — from cooking trays of bacon in restaurant ovens to baking dozens of cookies, pies and loaves of bread at a time. For family meals, I use the multiple racks so that even dessert cooks along with the main course. When cooking for potlucks or picnics, I make several items and freeze some for later use.

The recipes in this book have been selected and developed to make the most of the convection oven. Gratins and casseroles cook quickly with crisp, golden toppings; roasts and poultry brown quickly on the outside while the interior remains moist and juicy; pizzas, breads, pies and cookies bake evenly; meringues dry perfectly. The convection oven also reheats and warms foods more quickly than a standard oven, and it provides a finishing touch for dishes that require quick browning after being precooked on the stove or in the microwave.

The best way to become familiar with your convection oven is to turn it to convection and cook something. Read the About Convection Cooking section in this book, consult your manufacturer's manual and start cooking. Try a simple roast turkey or chicken (pages 58 or 173) or a batch of muffins or cookies (pages 131 to 141). Or make one of your family's favorites by following the simple guidelines for adapting standard recipes to convection cooking (page 14).

You'll quickly become comfortable with the features and potential of your oven, and you will never roast a chicken the old way again.

About Convection Cooking

IN CONVECTION COOKING, HEATED AIR IS CONTINUOUSLY circulated throughout the oven by a fan located at the rear of the oven. This provides even heat distribution for faster and more even cooking and browning. There may be several heating elements, depending on the model. Sometimes these elements are hidden, which allows easy cleaning. The heated air surrounds and penetrates food from every angle, sealing in natural moisture and flavors. Convection cooking also saves time and energy. Most foods can be cooked at lower temperatures and/or in less time than in a standard oven.

There are many different manufacturers of convection ovens, and not all ovens offer identical features. Most home models combine a standard oven with convection options. Some ovens have three cooking modes (bake, broil and convection), while others have up to five (bake, broil, convection bake, convection roast and convection broil). Some larger semi-commercial ovens have only the convection mode.

Multiple racks and rack settings can be used, which means several batches (up to six trays of cookies in some ovens) or several different dishes can be cooked at the same time (some ovens feature racks with rollers, for easy adjusting). In the convection oven, food smells tend not to be transferred from one dish to another, so you can even cook fish and a dessert at the same time.

The following information highlights the features and suggested uses for the convection settings. Element usage may vary depending on the make of your oven. For further information and suggestions, always consult your manufacturer's manual before using your oven.

Oven Settings
Convection Bake

In convection baking, the convection/rear element and fan operate (in some models the bottom element also operates). Use the convection bake setting for cakes, soufflés, cookies, pastries, breads and casseroles. If your oven has only one convection setting, it is most similar to the convection bake mode. You can also roast meat and poultry successfully on this setting. Record the mode, temperature and cooking time on your recipes for future reference.

To convection bake, preheat the oven until the indicator light goes off. Some ovens chime to indicate that the oven has come to temperature. In many ovens, the fan will stop whenever the door is opened.

Recommended Safe Temperatures for Doneness

Beef and Lamb	140°F (60°C) rare to medium-rare
	160°F (70°C) medium
	170°F (75°C) well done
Pork	160°F (70°C) medium
Ground Beef and Pork	170°F (75°C) well done
Ham (ready to eat and fully cooked)	140°F (60°C)
Whole Chicken and Turkey (unstuffed)*	180°F (82°C)
Turkey Breast	170°F (75°C)
Ground Chicken and Turkey	175°F (80°C)

* **Do not stuff whole poultry to be cooked in the convection oven. Because of the shorter cooking time, the meat may be cooked before the stuffing reaches a safe temperature.**

Convection Roast

In convection roasting, the top and/or bottom element(s) may come on in addition to the convection/rear element and fan. The additional heat source helps to brown foods. If you have a convection roast setting on your oven, use it for roasting meats and poultry. Some manufacturers recommend using the roast function for certain pies and pastries and some do not (ovens that employ the top element while roasting may cause pastry to brown too quickly). Check your manual.

Convection cooking is excellent for roasting; meat is seared or browned quickly on the outside while the interior remains tender and juicy. Adjust the racks so that the top of the meat is in the center of the oven.

Most meats are cooked on a rack set over a broiler pan for easier air circulation around the food, allowing for better browning. Many ovens come with these broiler pan/racks but you can also make your own by placing a wire rack or roasting rack over a pan with shallow sides.

The roasting times given in the recipes in this book are guidelines. The best way to make sure that meat is cooked safely and to your likeness is to use a meat thermometer. Several kinds are available: the meat probe that comes with the oven, the digital thermometer, the instant-read thermometer, the ovenproof thermometer, the fork thermometer and pop-up indicators. Some thermometers stay in foods while they cook; others do not. Insert the thermometer stem into the thickest part of the food, not touching bone, fat or gristle. Always wash the thermometer stem in hot soapy water after use.

Roasts should be allowed to stand for 5 to 15 minutes before carving. This allows the juices to retract and makes carving easier; the internal temperature also continues to rise after the meat comes out of the oven. When timing your meal service, be sure to incorporate resting time.

The recipes in this book start with a preheated oven, though not all manufacturers suggest preheating when cooking larger pieces of meat such as roasts and whole turkeys and chickens, so consult your manual.

If your oven does not have a convection roast function, just use the convection setting. The cooking time may be slightly longer than the time suggested in the recipe.

Convection Broil

In convection broiling, the top element(s) heat while the fan circulates air. This feature varies in different makes of ovens. Some broilers are preset (e.g., at 450°F/230°C) while others require setting. Not all manufacturers recommend preheating the broiler. Some recommend leaving the oven door open; others keeping it closed. Check your oven manual.

Adjust the rack position before broiling. Most recipes in this book call for the top of the food to be placed about 4 inches (10 cm) from the heat. In general, the thicker the food, the farther it is placed from the heat source. If you are broiling meat, trim off any excess fat to prevent splattering. Try to turn foods only once for even cooking.

If your oven does not have a convection broil function, simply use your standard broiler. The results will be similar, though the cooking time may be slightly longer with the standard broiler.

Converting and Adapting Recipes

Here are general guidelines for adapting standard recipes to the convection oven:

- Bake at the same temperature for 25% less time *or* reduce the oven temperature 25°F (13°C) and bake for the same time as the recipe suggests. Always check before the end of the cooking time for doneness. This will depend on what you are cooking. For cakes start checking 10 minutes before the end of the cooking time; for a large roast turkey start checking 40 minutes ahead of the suggested time. (Foods cooked in covered dishes or wrapped in foil will not benefit from the circulating air of the convection function, but covered dishes can be cooked at the same time as convection oven recipes.)

- If the recipe calls for a cooking time of less than 15 minutes (e.g., cookie recipes), reduce the oven temperature rather than reducing the cooking time. (The advantage of making cookies in the convection oven is that you can make several batches at once with even baking.)

- For very large cuts of meat and poultry, you may reduce the oven temperature 25°F to 50°F (13°C to 25°C) or reduce the cooking time by up to 30%. Check for doneness before the end of the suggested cooking time using a meat thermometer. The bonus of convection cooking is that the cooking time is reduced *and* the meat is roasted to a golden brown, sealing in flavorful juices. Note the new convection baking temperature and cooking time on your recipes.

Note: The recipes in this book can also be cooked in a standard oven. Simply increase the oven temperature by 25°F (13°C) or increase the cooking time by 25%.

Cookware and Containers

Few new cookware items and containers should be required for your convection oven. Keep in mind that the whole point of convection cooking is to have the heat circulating around food to produce golden and, in some cases, crispy finishing.

Here are a few guidelines:

- Lids and high-sided pans block the heat.
- Cookie sheets without sides allow heat to circulate around cookies. If you are using insulated (double-bottomed) cookie sheets, baking times may need to be increased.
- Metal baking pans conduct heat well. Dark metal absorbs heat, which is conducive to browning, while shiny metal reflects heat, giving a lighter finish.
- Glass or ceramic dishes do not conduct heat as well as metal, so there will be less browning or crisping on the sides and bottom. Use them for casserole or soufflés.
- Baking sheets with shallow sides encourage even browning on items such as roasted vegetables or appetizers.
- For roasting, use a broiler pan or shallow baking pan with a rack to elevate the meat. Roasting pans with high sides block the heat flow.
- Many recipes call for parchment (baking) paper, available in supermarkets and kitchen shops. Parchment paper is nonstick and heatproof and is used to line loaf pans, cake pans, cookie sheets and baking sheets. It prevents food from sticking, saves on clean-up time and cuts down on the need for additional fat to grease the pans. It can sometimes be reused.

- Foil is suggested for lining pans when food juices may run and caramelize. Do not let the foil block heat conduction or touch elements. Occasionally, recipes are covered for part of the cooking time to prevent food from browning too soon and to keep some steam in the dish.

General Tips

- Read the manufacturer's use and care manual before using your oven.
- Do not store items in the oven.
- Use dry pot holders (wet pot holders or oven mitts conduct heat and can cause steam burns).
- To keep the oven heat at a consistent temperature, use the interior light to check cooking progress rather than opening the door often.
- Open the door slowly to allow hot air or steam to escape before reaching in.
- For best results, position food in the center of the oven, leaving space around pans and trays for air to circulate. Stagger the placement of pans in the oven where possible.

Food Safety

- Wash your hands for 20 seconds before starting to cook and after coughing, sneezing, using the restroom and touching pets.
- Keep work surfaces, cutting boards and counter surfaces clean. Sanitize them with a mild chlorine bleach solution (especially when working with meats, poultry and seafood). Mix 1 tsp (5 mL) bleach with 3 cups (750 mL) water and store the bleach solution in a well-labeled spray bottle.
- Use two cutting boards: one for raw meat, poultry and fish; one for cooked foods, fresh vegetables and fruits.
- Keep cold foods cold, below 40°F (4°C).
- Keep hot foods hot, above 140°F (60°C).
- Keep raw meat, poultry and seafood separate from one another, other foods and cooked foods. Use clean utensils and dishes when switching from raw to cooked foods.
- Defrost meat, poultry and fish completely under refrigeration and keep in the refrigerator until cooking.
- Marinate foods in the refrigerator. Boil any remaining marinade for 7 minutes. Do not reuse raw marinades.
- Use a spoon instead of a brush to baste raw foods, as it is difficult to clean brushes thoroughly.
- Use a food/meat thermometer to check the internal temperature of foods.
- Refrigerate leftovers as quickly as possible. Cooling to room temperature on the counter invites bacteria growth. Use leftovers quickly.

About These Recipes

- The recipes in this book were tested in a variety of ovens — some with just the convection feature; others featuring convection bake, convection roast and convection broil. Always check your oven manual before cooking and make sure your oven temperature is calibrated correctly (manuals have directions for this). Make notes on your recipes re setting, temperature and cooking time. All ovens are not exactly the same.
- The following were used unless otherwise specified: regular table salt, freshly ground black pepper, salted butter, 2% milk and yogurt, homemade or canned stock (canned broth diluted according to package instructions).
- Always taste and adjust seasonings at the end of the cooking time.
- Certain recipes can be prepared to a point, covered and refrigerated. For good finishing results, it is recommended that the dish stand for up to 30 minutes at room temperature (68° to 70°F/19° to 20°C) before final baking or reheating to take off some refrigerator chill.

Convection Toaster Ovens

Convection toaster ovens bake, broil and toast. As with large convection ovens, hot air is circulated around the food while it cooks. Smaller than standard floor or wall ovens, convection toaster ovens sit on a heatproof counter surface, taking up minimal space, so they are ideal for cottages, chalets and recreational vehicles. (Check your manual for suggestions about counter placement, use and care.) They are less expensive than large kitchen stove/ovens, but more expensive than standard toaster ovens. They can serve as the only oven for students and singles, occasional cooks or retirees with small kitchens. They can also serve as a second oven when you are preparing smaller quantities of food or when you need extra oven space.

Most convection toaster ovens have both standard and convection functions. Most offer toaster and broiler options. The ovens are usually equipped with an oven rack and a combination broiler rack with oven pan (also called a drip tray or bake pan). The oven pan doubles as a baking sheet.

Use caution when lining a pan or dish with parchment paper in the convection toaster oven. Do not let the paper extend beyond the pan edges, as grease can accumulate, causing flareups. Most manufacturers do not recommend using foil in the convection toaster oven.

To convert recipes from the standard oven, use the same temperature; the cooking time may be slightly shorter (check 5 to 20 minutes before the end of the cooking time, depending on the item being cooked). If you are cooking a convection oven recipe (such as the ones in this book) in a convection toaster oven, increase the temperature by 25°F (13°C) (e.g., if the recipe calls for a temperature of 325°F/160°C in the regular convection oven, increase the temperature to 350°F/180°C if you are making the same dish in the convection toaster oven).

Select baking pans and casserole dishes that fit easily in your convection toaster oven, leaving at least 1-inch (2.5 cm) space for air to circulate. Use shallow-sided baking pans to allow for even heat distribution. (Make sure your pan fits before you start making the recipe!)

The toaster oven recipes in this book highlight the oven's versatility — from appetizers and main courses to desserts. Meals can easily be rounded out with a simple salad, steamed vegetable and a potato or rice dish.

If you want to make your favorite recipes in the convection toaster oven, the most important consideration will be container size. Consult the recipes and suggestions in your oven manual. You may need to adjust the quantities and yields to adapt recipes to the smaller oven.

Appetizers and Soups

Airplane Snacks 20

Savory Shortbread Bites 21

Apricot Prosciutto Wraps 22

French Onion Soup Bruschetta 23

Tomato Basil Pizzettes 24

Camembert Pesto Phyllo Cups 25

Chicken Satay Quesadillas 26

Eggplant Olive Tapenade 27

Ham and Cheese Quesadillas 28

Salsa Nachos 29

Southwestern Wings 30

Squash and Parsnip Soup 31

Roasted Tomato and Garlic Soup 32

Airplane Snacks

MAKES ABOUT
11 CUPS (2.75 L)

When I accompanied a tour group to Thailand, I prepared goody bags that contained bottled water, small spritz bottles (for cooling down), towelettes, note pads and these treats to eat on the plane. Some snacks almost made it to Thailand.

Roasted chickpeas can be found in bulk food stores.

Make Ahead
Snacks can be prepared two weeks in advance. For traveling, pack in small plastic bags or storage containers.

2 cups	wheat square cereal	500 mL
2 cups	toasted o-shaped cereal	500 mL
1 cup	pretzel sticks	250 mL
1 cup	roasted chickpeas	250 mL
1 cup	roasted peanuts or cashews	250 mL
1 cup	whole almonds or pecan halves	250 mL
½ cup	unsalted sunflower seeds	125 mL
½ cup	maple syrup or corn syrup	125 mL
1 tbsp	Worcestershire sauce	15 mL
1½ tsp	curry powder	7 mL
1 tsp	garlic salt or garlic powder	5 mL
½ tsp	dried thyme leaves	2 mL
½ tsp	salt	2 mL
¼ tsp	cayenne pepper	1 mL
¼ tsp	black pepper	1 mL
1 cup	golden raisins	250 mL
1 cup	dried cranberries	250 mL

1. In a large bowl, combine cereals, pretzel sticks, chickpeas, peanuts, almonds and sunflower seeds.
2. In a small saucepan, combine maple syrup, Worcestershire, curry powder, garlic salt, thyme, salt, cayenne and pepper. Heat over medium heat until warm. Pour over cereal and nuts. Toss well.
3. Spoon mixture onto two parchment-lined baking sheets. Convection bake in a preheated 225°F (110°C) oven for 30 to 35 minutes, or until golden and dry. Stir occasionally during toasting.
4. Let mixture cool and transfer to bowl. Stir in raisins and cranberries. Store in an airtight container at room temperature.

Savory Shortbread Bites

**MAKES ABOUT
6½ DOZEN**

These bites can be served as an alternative to nuts and chips. Attractively packaged and labeled, they make a nice addition to a gift basket. They can also be sprinkled over salads or soups.

Make Ahead
These bites can be made ahead, stored in an airtight container and frozen for up to three weeks.

1 cup	all-purpose flour	250 mL
¼ cup	grated Parmesan cheese	50 mL
¼ tsp	curry powder	1 mL
¼ tsp	ground cumin	1 mL
¼ tsp	cayenne pepper	1 mL
½ cup	butter, softened	125 mL
2 tbsp	granulated sugar	25 mL
1 tbsp	paprika	15 mL
1 tbsp	coarse salt	15 mL

1. In a bowl, combine flour, cheese, curry powder, cumin and cayenne.

2. In a separate bowl, cream together butter and sugar until light. Stir in dry ingredients and combine just until blended.

3. Divide dough into four equal pieces. Wrap in plastic wrap and refrigerate for 30 minutes.

4. Sprinkle paprika and salt over cutting board or counter. Roll each piece of dough into a 14-inch (34 cm) rope on paprika mixture. Cut into ½-inch (5 cm) pieces. Place on two parchment-lined baking sheets. Repeat with remaining ropes.

5. Convection bake in a preheated 325°F (160°C) oven for 12 to 15 minutes, or until golden. Cool completely before storing.

Apricot Prosciutto Wraps

MAKES 20 PIECES

This last-minute appetizer can be a sanity saver, especially during the holiday season. For variety you can use dried prunes, dates or figs instead of apricots. Guests often don't realize how much they enjoy dried fruit until they try this salty-sweet combination.

20	dried apricots	20
½ cup	orange juice or apple juice	125 mL
½ tsp	dried rosemary leaves	2 mL
6 to 7	thin slices prosciutto, cut lengthwise in 3 or 4 strips	6 to 7

1. In a small saucepan, combine apricots, orange juice and rosemary. Bring to a boil. Cover and remove from heat. Let stand for 20 minutes, or until apricots have softened. Stir occasionally.

2. Wrap each apricot with a prosciutto strip (use toothpicks if you wish). Place on a parchment-lined baking sheet. Convection bake in a preheated 400°F (200°C) oven for 6 to 8 minutes, or until prosciutto is slightly crisp. Serve warm.

Casual Appetizer Party for 6 to 8

All these recipes can easily be doubled or tripled to serve a larger crowd. Make the Airplane Snacks and shortbread ahead. The other appetizers can be baked together and served hot or at room temperature. Round out the serving table with an assortment of cheeses, fresh fruit and vegetables and bowls of nuts.

- Airplane Snacks (page 20)
- Savory Shortbread Bites (page 21)
- Tomato and Basil Pizzettes (page 24)
- Ham and Cheese Quesadillas (page 28)
- Southwestern Wings (page 30)
- Apricot Prosciutto Wraps (page 22)

French Onion Soup Bruschetta

MAKES 12 TO
14 BRUSCHETTA

These bruschetta provide the rich, sweet flavor of French onion soup, without the broth. Float them on top of soup or use the caramelized onions as a topping for baked potatoes (top potatoes with the onions and cheese and return to the oven for 5 minutes, or until the cheese melts). The cheese could also be replaced with ½ cup (125 mL) chopped black or green olives or roasted red peppers.

Make Ahead
The onions can be cooked ahead, covered and refrigerated for up to two days.

2	small Spanish or sweet onions, quartered and thinly sliced (about 1½ lb/750 g)	2
1 cup	dry white wine, chicken stock or vegetable stock	250 mL
3 tbsp	olive oil	45 mL
½ tsp	herbes de Provence or dried thyme leaves	2 mL
½ tsp	salt	2 mL
¼ tsp	black pepper	1 mL
12 to 14	diagonal slices baguette (thin French stick), about ½ inch (1 cm) thick	12 to 14
¾ cup	grated Gruyère cheese	175 mL

1. Combine onions, wine, olive oil, herbes de Provence, salt and pepper on a parchment-lined baking sheet. Convection bake in a preheated 400°F (200°C) oven for 35 to 40 minutes, or until onions are golden and liquid has evaporated. Stir onions several times during baking. Cool to room temperature.

2. Turn off oven and preheat broiler. Arrange bread slices on a baking sheet and place about 4 inches (10 cm) from heat. Convection broil for 1 to 2 minutes per side, or until lightly toasted.

3. Turn bread slices. Divide onion mixture evenly over bread. Top with cheese. Broil for 2 to 3 minutes, or until cheese has just melted.

Herbes de Provence
A blend of dried herbs from Provence, usually including thyme, rosemary, summer savory and marjoram. Other herbs such as oregano, basil, lavender, parsley and chervil may also be included.

Tomato Basil Pizzettes

MAKES
4 MINI PIZZAS

These mini pizzas are quick to assemble as a snack or light lunch with a salad. Use a variety of tomatoes when they are in season — try the yellow varieties and even halved cherry tomatoes.

4	6-inch (15 cm) flour tortillas	4
1½ cups	grated mozzarella cheese	375 mL
1	large tomato, halved lengthwise, cored and thinly sliced	1
6	fresh basil leaves, finely shredded	6
2 tbsp	grated Parmesan cheese	25 mL
2 tbsp	olive oil	25 mL

1. Arrange tortillas on a baking sheet. Divide mozzarella evenly over tortillas and spread almost to edges. Arrange tomato slices over cheese. Sprinkle with basil and Parmesan. Drizzle with olive oil.

2. Convection bake in a preheated 400°F (200°C) oven for 6 to 8 minutes, or until cheese is bubbling. Serve pizzas whole or cut in quarters.

Celebration Dinner for 6

Make the phyllo cups, pastry for the Napoleons and roasted pears and candied pecans ahead of time. Add the cheese to the phyllo cups and heat just before serving. While guests are eating the appetizer and salad, cook the salmon, rice and vegetables. Assemble the Napoleons just before serving.

- Camembert Pesto Phyllo Cups (page 25)
- Roasted Pear Salad with Candied Pecans and Blue Cheese (page 110)
- Maple-glazed Salmon (page 34)
- Steamed Rice
- Sautéed Broccoli or Green Beans
- Lemon and White Chocolate Napoleons (page 152)

Camembert Pesto Phyllo Cups

MAKES 24 CUPS

Phyllo pastry bakes to golden perfection in the convection oven. Vary the filling by using other cheeses such as Brie, mozzarella or Cambozola.

Make Ahead
Bake phyllo cups, remove from pans, cool and freeze in an airtight container for up to two weeks. To reheat, return to muffin pans or simply place on baking sheet and continue with Step 5.

2	sheets phyllo pastry	2
4 tsp	olive oil, divided	15 mL
6 oz	Camembert, cut in 1/2-inch (1 cm) pieces (about 24 pieces)	175 g
1/4 cup	pesto, storebought or homemade (page 124)	50 mL

1. Place a sheet of phyllo pastry on a flat surface. Brush with 2 tsp (10 mL) olive oil. Top with remaining sheet of phyllo and brush with remaining 2 tsp (10 mL) oil.

2. Using a ruler and sharp knife, cut phyllo into 48 2-inch (5 cm) squares (cut 8 squares along long side and 6 squares down width).

3. Press half the squares into two mini muffin pans. Press remaining phyllo squares on top of first squares at an angle.

4. Convection bake or roast in a preheated 300°F (150°C) oven for 6 minutes, or until golden. Remove from oven and let sit for 5 minutes.

5. Place a piece of cheese in each cup. Top with 1/2 tsp (2 mL) pesto. Return to oven for 5 to 6 minutes, or until cheese has melted. Serve warm.

Chicken Satay Quesadillas

MAKES 24 PIECES

When I was a caterer, the most popular appetizers were mini chicken satays and quesadillas, so for this recipe I have combined the two. Leftover cooked turkey also works well. Serve these as appetizers or for lunch accompanied by sliced cucumber, carrots and sweet Asian chili sauce — a sweet, spicy condiment available in Asian groceries and most supermarkets.

If you are using storebought peanut sauce, select one that is not too runny (it should be almost the consistency of mayonnaise).

6	9-inch (23 cm) flour tortillas	6
¾ cup	peanut sauce, storebought or homemade	175 mL
2 cups	grated mozzarella or Gruyère cheese	500 mL
2 cups	diced cooked chicken	500 mL
3	green onions, finely chopped	3
¼ cup	chopped fresh cilantro	50 mL

1. Place tortillas on a flat surface. Spread half of each tortilla with peanut sauce. Sprinkle with cheese, chicken, green onions and cilantro. Fold tortillas in half and press firmly.

2. Arrange tortillas on two parchment-lined baking sheets. Convection bake in a preheated 400°F (200°C) oven for 6 to 7 minutes or until cheese melts and quesadillas are heated through. Let stand for 4 minutes, then cut each tortilla into 4 wedges.

Peanut Sauce

In a small skillet, heat 2 tbsp (25 mL) vegetable oil over medium heat. Add 2 tbsp (25 mL) chopped gingerroot, 2 chopped cloves garlic and 4 chopped green onions. Cook for 2 minutes until softened.

In a food processor or blender, combine cooled ginger mixture, ½ cup (125 mL) peanut butter, ½ cup (125 mL) coconut milk, ¼ cup (50 mL) chopped fresh cilantro, 2 tbsp (25 mL) soy sauce, 2 tbsp (25 mL) lime juice, 1 tbsp (15 mL) fish sauce, 1 tbsp (15 mL) packed brown sugar and ½ tsp (2 mL) hot chili sauce. Blend until smooth. Makes about 1½ cups (375 mL).

Eggplant Olive Tapenade

MAKES
1½ CUPS (375 ML)

This spread combines the flavors of eggplant caviar (a mixture of roasted eggplant, tomatoes and seasonings) and tapenade (a savory Provençal spread of black olives, anchovies and capers). Serve with thinly sliced bread, raw vegetables or as a condiment with roast chicken or lamb. Sometimes I spoon the mixture into small hollowed-out tomatoes to serve as part of a buffet. For a vegetarian version, simply omit the anchovies.

Make Ahead
The tapenade can be prepared, covered and refrigerated up to one day ahead.

1	large eggplant (about 1¼ lbs/625 g)	1
¾ cup	pitted black or green olives	175 mL
2	cloves garlic, chopped	2
2	anchovy fillets, chopped	2
2 tbsp	capers	25 mL
2 tsp	chopped fresh thyme, or ½ tsp (2 mL) dried	10 mL
¼ cup	olive oil	50 mL
¼ tsp	black pepper	1 mL
2 tbsp	chopped fresh basil or parsley	25 mL

1. Pierce eggplant with a fork. Place on a foil-lined baking sheet and convection bake in a preheated 400°F (200°C) oven for 40 to 45 minutes, or until eggplant is soft and starting to collapse.

2. When eggplant is cool enough to handle, cut in half. Scoop out pulp.

3. Place olives, garlic, anchovies and capers in food processor. Process until coarsely chopped. Add eggplant pulp and thyme. Process until blended but not pureed.

4. Add olive oil and pepper. Pulse to combine.

5. Spoon into a serving bowl and garnish with chopped basil.

Ham and Cheese Quesadillas

MAKES 18
TO 24 PIECES

An updated version of the grilled ham and cheese sandwich, these quesadillas can be served as a light main course or as an appetizer. Serve them with sour cream and salsa.

Make Ahead
Prepare and bake quesadillas, wrap and freeze for up to two weeks.
To reheat directly from frozen state, convection bake at 350°F (180 °C) for 10 to 12 minutes, or until hot.

¾ cup	grated Cheddar cheese	175 mL
½ cup	chili sauce or tomato salsa	125 mL
2 tsp	coarse-grain or Russian-style mustard	10 mL
6	6-inch (15 cm) flour tortillas	6
3	large slices Black Forest ham	3

1. In a bowl, combine cheese, chili sauce and mustard.

2. Arrange three tortillas on a flat surface. Divide half of cheese mixture among tortillas and spread evenly, leaving a 1-inch (2.5 cm) border around edges.

3. Top cheese with ham slices and spread evenly with remaining cheese. Top with remaining tortillas. Press down slightly.

4. Arrange quesadillas on a parchment-lined baking sheet. Convection bake in a preheated 400°F (200°C) oven for 10 minutes, or until cheese melts and quesadillas are heated through. Cool for 5 minutes before cutting each quesadilla into 6 to 8 wedges.

Variation
Black Bean and Cheese Quesadillas: Combine 1 cup (250 mL) canned black beans (drained and rinsed), ¼ cup (50 mL) chopped fresh cilantro and ¼ tsp (1 mL) ground cumin. Replace ham with bean mixture.

Salsa Nachos

MAKES 4
TO 6 SERVINGS

A favorite snack for
all ages. For a less
spicy version, use a
mild salsa and reduce
the green chilies. Some
canned green chilies are
not spicy; the jalapeños
are. Serve with a side
dish of guacamole.

1 cup	tomato salsa	250 mL
¼ cup	diced canned green chilies, or 2 fresh jalapeños, seeded and finely chopped	50 mL
¼ cup	chopped green onion	50 mL
4 cups	tortilla chips	1 L
2 cups	grated Monterey Jack or Cheddar cheese (8 oz/250 g), divided	500 mL
2 tbsp	chopped fresh cilantro	25 mL
¼ cup	sour cream	50 mL

1. In a small bowl, combine salsa, chilies and green onions.
2. Spread tortilla chips over a 13- by 9-inch (3 L) baking dish. Sprinkle chips with 1 cup (250 mL) cheese. Spoon salsa over cheese and top with remaining 1 cup (250 mL) cheese.
3. Convection bake in a preheated 425°F (220°C) oven for 3 to 4 minutes, or until cheese is bubbly. Top with cilantro and dollops of sour cream.

Guacamole
Scoop flesh of 2 ripe avocados into a bowl and mash coarsely. Add 2 finely chopped green onions, 2 tbsp (25 mL) lime juice or lemon juice, ½ tsp (2 mL) chili powder, ⅓ cup (75 mL) tomato salsa, 1 minced clove garlic and 3 tbsp (45 mL) chopped fresh cilantro. Mix thoroughly. Makes about 1½ cups (375 mL).

Southwestern Wings

MAKES 30 TO
34 WINGS, ABOUT
4 TO 5 SERVINGS

A must for chicken-wing
fans. If you are
serving a crowd, double
or triple the recipe.
Cooking the wings in
the convection oven on
a wire rack makes them
crispy all over. If a rack
is not available, simply
arrange the wings on a
foil-lined baking sheet.

Serve the wings with
salsa, a dip or sour cream
sprinkled with cilantro.

3 lbs	chicken wings	1.5 kg
¼ cup	cornmeal	50 mL
2 tbsp	all-purpose flour	25 mL
2 tsp	chili powder	10 mL
1 tsp	ground cumin	5 mL
1 tsp	garlic powder	5 mL
1 tsp	salt	5 mL
½ tsp	dried thyme leaves	2 mL
½ tsp	cayenne pepper	2 mL

1. Trim off wing tips (freeze tips and reserve to make stock).
   Cut each wing into two pieces at the joint.

2. In a large bowl, combine cornmeal, flour, chili powder,
   cumin, garlic powder, salt, thyme and cayenne. Toss
   wings in mixture to coat. Arrange wings "good" side up
   on wire rack placed over a foil-lined baking sheet.

3. Convection bake in a preheated 400°F (200°C) oven
   for 35 to 40 minutes, or until wings are cooked through,
   crisp and golden.

Savory Dip
In a bowl, combine ½ cup (125 mL) mayonnaise,
2 tbsp (25 mL) finely chopped green onion,
2 tbsp (25 mL) finely chopped dill pickle,
1 tbsp (15 mL) chopped capers, 1 tbsp (15 mL)
lemon juice, 1 tsp (5 mL) coarse-grain mustard,
½ tsp (2 mL) dried tarragon leaves, ¼ tsp (1 mL) salt
and ¼ tsp (1 mL) black pepper. Makes about ¾ cup
(175 mL).

Squash and Parsnip Soup

MAKES 5 SERVINGS

Roasting the vegetables gives this soup a rich flavor without adding cream. Sweet potatoes could be substituted for the squash. For variety, use blue cheese, goat cheese or Cheddar as a garnish.

Make Ahead

Soup can be prepared, covered and refrigerated for up to two days or frozen for up to two months. Onion garnish can be prepared ahead, covered and refrigerated for up to two days.

1	butternut squash (about 2 lbs/1 kg)	1
4	parsnips (about 1 lb/500 g total)	4
2 tbsp	olive oil	25 mL
1	onion, peeled and cut in 8 pieces	1
2 tsp	chopped fresh sage, or 1/2 tsp (2 mL) dried	10 mL
5 cups	vegetable stock or chicken stock	1.25 L
1/2 tsp	salt	2 mL
1/4 tsp	black pepper	1 mL

GARNISH

2 tbsp	olive oil	25 mL
1	onion, thinly sliced	1
	Salt and black pepper to taste	

1. Peel squash and remove seeds. Peel parsnips. Cut squash and parsnips into 1/2-inch (1 cm) pieces. Arrange in a 13- by 9-inch (3 L) baking dish. Drizzle with oil and toss.

2. Convection bake or roast in a preheated 375°F (190°C) oven for 25 minutes. Stir in onion and sage. Continue to roast for 20 to 30 minutes, or until vegetables are tender. Stir several times during roasting. Remove from oven and let sit for 10 minutes.

3. Transfer vegetables to a food processor and puree until smooth (you may have to do this in batches).

4. In a large saucepan, combine stock, pureed vegetables, salt and pepper (if using an immersion blender, add vegetables directly to stock and puree). Bring soup to a boil. Reduce heat and simmer for 10 minutes.

5. For the garnish, heat oil in a medium skillet over medium-high heat. Add sliced onion and cook, stirring often, for 5 to 10 minutes, or until caramelized. Season with salt and pepper. Spoon onions over soup.

Roasted Tomato and Garlic Soup

MAKES 5
TO 6 SERVINGS

When tomatoes are plentiful, make several batches of this versatile soup to freeze. Choose the ripest tomatoes. You can also serve this chilled, with a squeeze of lime juice, diced cucumber, red pepper or avocado. For a hot, creamy soup, add ½ cup (125 mL) whipping cream and heat before serving. Additional garnishes might be chopped fresh dillweed, basil or pesto.

Make Ahead
Soup can be cooked, covered and refrigerated for up to two days or frozen for up to two months.

2 lbs	tomatoes, cored and halved (about 6 medium)	1 kg
2	onions, peeled and cut in 8 pieces	2
6	whole cloves garlic, peeled and halved	6
2 tbsp	olive oil	25 mL
½ tsp	salt	2 mL
¼ tsp	black pepper	1 mL
3 cups	vegetable stock or chicken stock	750 mL

1. In a 13- by 9-inch (3 L) baking dish, combine tomatoes, onions, garlic and olive oil. Sprinkle with salt and pepper. Convection bake or roast in a preheated 375°F (190°C) oven for 35 minutes. Stir occasionally. Let tomatoes cool slightly and slip off skins.

2. Puree vegetables with juices in a food processor or blender until smooth. Transfer to a saucepan and add stock (if you are using an immersion blender, transfer roasted vegetables directly to saucepan with stock and puree). Bring to a boil on high heat. Reduce heat to medium and simmer for 10 minutes, until slightly thickened. Taste and adjust seasonings if necessary.

Avocados
A ripe avocado should yield gently to finger pressure. If the avocado is not quite ripe, leave it at room temperature, checking each day. Just before serving, halve the avocado and twist slightly. Remove the pit, then peel and slice the pulp.

Mom's Salmon Loaf (page 36)

Fish and Seafood

Maple-glazed Salmon *34*

Hoisin Orange Salmon *35*

Mom's Salmon Loaf *36*

Lemon and Dill Fish Kabobs *37*

Red Snapper with Herbed Bread Crumbs
and Tartar Sauce *38*

Tilapia Mexicana *40*

Baked Cod with Pistou *41*

Fish Fillets with Miso Dressing *42*

Fish Cakes *43*

Shrimp with Tomato and Feta *44*

Chicken Souvlaki with Tzatziki (page 52) and Summer Peppers (page 98)

Maple-glazed Salmon

MAKES 6 SERVINGS

I came up with this simple recipe when faced with an extra piece of salmon and little preparation time. It is a great choice for a quick cottage meal or to serve cold on a buffet.

You can also use trout, salmon trout or Arctic char in this recipe.

¼ cup	maple syrup	50 mL
4 tsp	coarse-grain mustard	20 mL
4 tsp	soy sauce	20 mL
2 lbs	salmon fillet, skin removed	1 kg

1. In a small bowl, combine maple syrup, mustard and soy sauce.
2. Arrange salmon on a foil- *and* parchment-lined baking sheet (for easy cleanup). Spoon glaze over fish.
3. Convection bake in a preheated 400°F (200°C) oven for 8 to 10 minutes, or until flesh just flakes easily with a fork. Do not overcook. Transfer fish to a serving platter using large lifters.

Mustards
Dry mustard is made from ground mustard seeds. It can be added to dishes as a seasoning or mixed with cold water to form a paste. It is hotter than Dijon or Russian-style mustard and is generally used sparingly. **Dijon mustard** can be smooth or **coarse-grain** (coarse-grain mustard adds texture to a dish as well as taste). It is used as a condiment or seasoning and usually contains white wine and/or vinegar, spices and salt. **Russian-style** or "honey mustard" is usually a smooth mustard with a sweet-sour flavor.

You can also experiment with the many novelty mustards that are now available, from maple flavored to wasabi lime.

Hoisin Orange Salmon

Quick, easy, full-flavored dishes are a welcome addition to any cook's repertoire. Look for hoisin sauce in the Asian section of the supermarket. Refrigerate it after opening. Other fish choices might be sea bass, halibut or monkfish.

Serve with a cucumber salad.

3 tbsp	hoisin sauce	45 mL
2 tbsp	orange juice concentrate, defrosted	25 mL
2 tsp	sesame oil	10 mL
2 tsp	finely chopped gingerroot	10 mL
6	6-oz (175 g) salmon fillets, skin removed	6
6	orange slices	6

1. In a small bowl, combine hoisin, orange juice concentrate, sesame oil and ginger.

2. Arrange salmon on a parchment-lined baking sheet. Spoon glaze over salmon, turning fillets to coat completely.

3. Convection bake in a preheated 400°F (200°C) oven for 8 to 10 minutes, or until fish flakes easily when tested with a fork. Garnish with orange slices.

Cucumber Salad
In a large bowl, combine 1 thinly sliced cucumber, 2 chopped green onions, 3 tbsp (45 mL) rice vinegar, 1 tsp (5 mL) granulated sugar and a pinch of salt. Let stand at room temperature for 20 minutes, tossing occasionally. Makes about 2 cups (500 mL).

Mom's Salmon Loaf

MAKES 4
TO 5 SERVINGS

In a weekly column that
I write for the local
newspaper, I included
this recipe under the title
"Post Holiday Simplicity"
in an article that
appeared the first week
after New Year's, when
everyone had overdosed
on holiday foods. Serve
it cold as part of a salad
dinner or hot with baked
potatoes or rice pilaf.

Make Ahead
Salmon loaf can be
cooked, unmolded,
covered and refrigerated
up to a day ahead.
Serve cold.

2	7½-oz (213 g) cans salmon, with juices	2
2	eggs	2
¾ cup	fresh bread crumbs	175 mL
½ cup	mayonnaise	125 mL
⅓ cup	chopped sweet pickle	75 mL
¼ cup	chopped celery	50 mL
2 tbsp	lemon juice	25 mL
¼ tsp	salt	1 mL
¼ tsp	black pepper	1 mL

1. In a large bowl, break up salmon and mash bones. Add eggs, bread crumbs, mayonnaise, pickle, celery, lemon juice, salt and pepper. Mix together thoroughly. Spoon into a parchment-lined or greased 8- by 4-inch (1.5 L) loaf pan.

2. Convection bake in a preheated 325°F (160°C) oven for 35 to 40 minutes, or until center is firm and top is golden. If cooking salmon loaf for later use, let rest in pan for 25 minutes before turning out (loosen edges with knife but for sure results, line pan with parchment paper). If serving hot, let stand for 5 minutes before slicing.

Roasted Cherry Tomatoes
In a medium bowl, combine 2 cups (500 mL) cherry tomatoes with 1 tbsp (15 mL) olive oil, ½ tsp (2 mL) granulated sugar, ¼ tsp (1 mL) salt and ¼ tsp (1 mL) pepper. Place in an 8-inch (2 L) square baking dish and convection bake in a preheated 325°F (160°C) oven for 10 minutes, or until just starting to soften. Makes 4 to 5 servings.

Lemon and Dill Fish Kabobs

MAKES 6 SERVINGS

You could also use chicken or vegetables such as zucchini and cherry tomatoes in this recipe. If you are using metal skewers, warn guests that they will be hot. Salmon and red peppers make an attractive combination, but yellow or green peppers can also be used. Serve with a rice pilaf or steamed new potatoes.

⅓ cup	lemon juice	75 mL
¼ cup	chopped fresh dillweed	50 mL
2 tbsp	olive oil	25 mL
1 tbsp	Russian-style mustard	15 mL
½ tsp	salt	2 mL
¼ tsp	black pepper	1 mL
2 lbs	salmon, halibut or cod, cut in 1-inch (2.5 cm) pieces	1 kg
1	large red bell pepper, seeded and cut in 1-inch (2.5 cm) pieces	1

1. In a large non-metallic bowl, combine lemon juice, dill, olive oil, mustard, salt and pepper.

2. Add fish to marinade and toss gently to coat. Marinate for 10 minutes.

3. Thread fish and pepper pieces onto six 6- to 8-inch (15 to 20 cm) skewers. Arrange on a lightly greased broiler pan. Spoon over any remaining marinade.

4. Place fish about 4 inches (10 cm) from the heat and convection broil under a preheated broiler for 4 minutes. Turn and cook for 4 to 5 minutes longer, or until fish flakes easily with a fork.

Red Snapper with Herbed Bread Crumbs and Tartar Sauce

MAKES 4 SERVINGS

The convection oven gives this gratin a crisp, golden topping, without overcooking the fish. You can substitute tilapia, grouper or trout for the red snapper. The tartar sauce can be served with any type of fish or used in sandwiches or potato salads.

Make Ahead
Tartar sauce can be made, covered and refrigerated up to one day ahead.

TARTAR SAUCE

¾ cup	mayonnaise	175 mL
2	green onions, finely chopped	2
¼ cup	chopped sweet or dill pickle	50 mL
2 tbsp	chopped fresh parsley	25 mL
1 tbsp	capers, chopped	15 mL
1 tbsp	lemon juice	15 mL
¼ tsp	salt	1 mL
¼ tsp	black pepper	1 mL

RED SNAPPER

4	6-oz (175 g) red snapper fillets	4
1 tbsp	olive oil	15 mL
1 tbsp	lemon juice	15 mL
¼ tsp	salt	1 mL
¼ tsp	black pepper	1 mL
1 cup	fresh bread crumbs	250 mL
¼ cup	chopped fresh dillweed	50 mL
¼ cup	grated Parmesan cheese	50 mL
2 tbsp	chopped fresh basil	25 mL
4 tsp	olive oil	20 mL

1. To prepare tartar sauce, in a bowl, combine mayonnaise, green onions, pickle, parsley, capers, lemon juice, salt and pepper in a bowl. Mix thoroughly. Cover and refrigerate.

2. Arrange snapper in a shallow baking dish just large enough to hold fish in a single layer.

3. In a small bowl or measuring cup, combine olive oil, lemon juice, salt and pepper. Pour marinade over fish, turning to coat fillets.

4. In a separate bowl, combine bread crumbs, dill, Parmesan, basil and olive oil. Sprinkle over fish and pat on.

5. Convection bake in a preheated 400°F (200°C) oven for 10 to 12 minutes, or until fish flakes easily with a fork and crumbs are golden. Serve with tartar sauce.

Fresh Bread Crumbs

Cut slightly stale bread into chunks and process in food processor until crumbs form. For finer crumbs, process until no large chunks remain. Freeze extra bread crumbs in freezer bags.

To dry bread crumbs, place on a baking sheet and convection bake in a preheated 275°F (140°C) oven for 10 to 15 minutes, or until dry. Turn off oven and leave crumbs in oven for 15 minutes. Cool at room temperature. Be sure crumbs are completely dry before storing. Dry bread crumbs can be stored in an airtight container at room temperature.

Panko bread crumbs are a good storebought substitute for homemade fresh or dry bread crumbs. They are large rice-shaped, dry white breadcrumbs and are often used in restaurants to give food a light, crunchy finish. They are now available in specialty food shops and some supermarkets.

Tilapia Mexicana

MAKES 4 SERVINGS

Tilapia is a mild and delicate fish that is readily available at supermarkets and fish shops. (You could also use red snapper or halibut in this recipe.)

This salad-like dish is similar to ceviche (where the fish is "cooked" in lime juice), but here the fish is baked before marinating. Serve with whole wheat bread (page 135) or warm flour tortillas.

1 tbsp	olive oil, divided	15 mL
1 lb	tilapia fillets	500 g
1/4 tsp	salt	1 mL
1/4 tsp	black pepper	1 mL

MARINADE

1/2 cup	lime juice	125 mL
1/3 cup	orange juice	75 mL
3 tbsp	olive oil	45 mL
2 tsp	grated orange zest	10 mL
1/4 tsp	hot pepper flakes	1 mL
1/2 tsp	salt	2 mL
1/4 tsp	black pepper	1 mL
1	small red onion, thinly sliced	1

GARNISH

1	red bell pepper, seeded and thinly sliced	1
1	orange, peeled and sliced	1
1	avocado, peeled and sliced	1
2 tbsp	chopped fresh cilantro or parsley	25 mL

1. Brush a 13- by 9-inch (3 L) baking dish with 1 tsp (5 mL) olive oil. Arrange fish in dish in a single layer, overlapping slightly if necessary. Drizzle with remaining 2 tsp (10 mL) oil. Season with salt and pepper. Convection bake in a preheated 350°F (180°C) oven for 8 minutes, or until just cooked. Let sit at room temperature for 20 minutes.

2. Meanwhile, to make marinade, in a small saucepan, combine lime juice, orange juice, olive oil, orange zest, pepper flakes, salt and pepper. Add onion slices. Bring to a boil and cook for 4 minutes. Remove from heat for 10 minutes, then pour over cooked fish.

3. Arrange red pepper and orange slices over fish. Cover and refrigerate for 2 to 4 hours, or until cool. Garnish with avocado and cilantro before serving.

Baked Cod with Pistou

MAKES 4 SERVINGS

Pistou is basically the Provençal version of pesto, without the pine nuts. If you have pesto on hand, it can be used instead. Very colorful and flavorful as a starter or simple lunch dish, this is also an excellent main course. Serve with roasted asparagus (page 77) and rice.

Make Ahead
Assemble dish completely. Cover with plastic and refrigerate for up to four hours before baking.

½ cup	packed fresh basil leaves	125 mL
1	clove garlic, chopped	1
3 tbsp	olive oil	45 mL
2 tbsp	grated Parmesan cheese	25 mL
½ tsp	salt	2 mL
¼ tsp	black pepper	1 mL
1 lb	cod, cut in 4 pieces	500 g
1	large tomato, halved lengthwise, cored and cut in 6 slices per side	1

1. To prepare pistou, place basil, garlic, olive oil, cheese, salt and pepper in food processor. Blend until smooth.

2. Arrange cod pieces in one layer on a parchment-lined baking sheet. Spoon pistou evenly over fish. Turn fish to coat in pistou. Place 3 tomato slices over each piece of fish.

3. Convection bake in a preheated 400°F (200°C) oven for 10 to 12 minutes, or until fish is opaque and just flakes with a fork.

Fish Fillets
with Miso Dressing

Miso, a fermented soybean paste, can be light or dark. The light- or medium-colored is the mildest and most popular. Found in Asian or health food stores in the refrigerated section, it is an everyday ingredient in Japanese cooking. Once opened, store miso tightly covered in the refrigerator.

This dish can also be served in smaller portions as a starter.

Make Ahead

Dressing can be prepared, covered and refrigerated up to two days ahead. For summer entertaining, cook the fish and pineapple up to a half hour in advance and serve at room temperature.

MISO DRESSING

2 tbsp	light miso	25 mL
2 tbsp	rice vinegar	25 mL
2 tbsp	pineapple juice or orange juice	25 mL
1	clove garlic, minced	1
1 tsp	liquid honey or granulated sugar	5 mL
2 tbsp	vegetable oil	25 mL
1 tbsp	sesame oil	15 mL

FISH

6	6-oz (175 g) salmon, sea bass or halibut fillets	6
1 tsp	grated lemon zest	5 mL
1 tbsp	sesame oil	15 mL
6	fresh pineapple slices	6
1 tbsp	toasted or black sesame seeds (optional)	15 mL
3	green onions, sliced on the diagonal	3

1. To prepare dressing, in a small bowl, whisk together miso, vinegar, pineapple juice, garlic, honey, vegetable oil and sesame oil.

2. Arrange fillets on a parchment-lined baking sheet. In a small bowl or cup, combine lemon zest and sesame oil. Spoon over fish. Roll fish to coat.

3. Arrange pineapple slices on a separate parchment-lined baking sheet. Convection bake fish and pineapple in a preheated 400°F (200°C) oven for 6 to 8 minutes, or until fish is opaque and flakes easily when tested with a fork.

4. To serve, place pineapple slices on individual serving plates. Place fish just slightly overlapping pineapple. Spoon dressing over fish. Garnish with sesame seeds, if using, and green onions.

Fish Cakes

MAKES 6 SERVINGS

Sometimes I even cook extra fish and potatoes, just so I can make these. Rather than being fried, these lower-fat fish cakes bake beautifully in the convection oven. Serve them as a starter (shape into smaller cakes), as a burger on a bun or as a main course with a spinach salad and tartar sauce (page 38).

1 lb	cooked fish (salmon, cod, crabmeat or a combination), flaked (about 2½ cups/625 mL)	500 g
2 cups	cooked mashed potatoes	500 mL
1	egg	1
½ cup	chopped celery	125 mL
¼ cup	chopped green onion	50 mL
¼ cup	mayonnaise	50 mL
2 tbsp	lemon juice	25 mL
2 tbsp	chopped fresh dillweed	25 mL
1 tsp	Dijon mustard	5 mL
¾ tsp	salt	4 mL
½ tsp	black pepper	2 mL
2 tbsp	melted butter or olive oil	25 mL

1. In a large bowl, combine fish, potatoes, egg, celery, green onion, mayonnaise, lemon juice, dill, mustard, salt and pepper. Mix thoroughly.

2. With dampened hands, shape mixture into 8 to 10 cakes. Arrange on a parchment-lined baking sheet or lightly greased broiler pan. Brush cakes with melted butter.

3. Convection bake in a preheated 400°F (200°C) oven for 20 to 22 minutes, or until cakes are golden brown.

Quick Spinach Salad

In a bowl, combine 6 cups (1.5 L) baby spinach leaves and 2 peeled and sectioned oranges. To make dressing, combine 4 tsp (20 mL) orange juice, 1 tbsp (15 mL) rice vinegar and 2 tsp (10 mL) sesame oil. Toss spinach and oranges with dressing. Sprinkle with 1 tbsp (15 mL) sesame seeds. Makes 4 to 6 servings.

Shrimp with Tomato and Feta

MAKES 4
TO 5 SERVINGS

Create your own
Mediterranean
holiday at home by
serving this dish as an
appetizer or main course
(serve with rice or lots
of crusty bread). The
Greek version would
use ouzo (a licorice-
flavored liqueur) in
place of the wine.

Make Ahead
Tomato sauce can be
prepared, covered and
refrigerated up to
one day earlier. Reheat
sauce on stove before
adding shrimp.

2 tbsp	olive oil	25 mL
2	onions, chopped	2
2	cloves garlic, finely chopped	2
1	28-oz (796 mL) can plum tomatoes, drained and chopped	1
1/2 cup	dry white wine	125 mL
1/4 cup	chopped fresh parsley	50 mL
1 tbsp	chopped fresh oregano or basil, or 1 tsp (5 mL) dried	15 mL
1/4 tsp	salt	1 mL
1/4 tsp	black pepper	1 mL
1 lb	shrimp, peeled, deveined and patted dry	500 g
1 cup	crumbled feta cheese (about 6 oz/175 g)	250 mL

1. In a large skillet, heat oil over medium-high heat. Add onions and garlic. Cook, stirring occasionally, for 4 minutes until softened but not colored. Add tomatoes, wine, parsley, oregano, salt and pepper. Cook until thickened but not too dry, about 8 minutes.

2. Remove from heat and add shrimp. Spoon into an 8-inch (2 L) square baking dish. Sprinkle feta over shrimp.

3. Convection bake in a preheated 325°F (160°C) oven for 22 to 25 minutes, or just until shrimp is pink. Let stand for a few minutes before serving.

Poultry

Roasted Flat Chicken *46*

Crispy Chicken with Cranberry Pear Relish *47*

Roasted Drumsticks and Vegetables *48*

Honey Garlic Chicken Wings *49*

Stuffed Chicken Breasts with Goat Cheese
and Red Pepper Sauce *50*

Chicken Souvlaki with Tzatziki *52*

Broiled Cilantro Garlic Chicken Breasts *53*

Cornish Hens with Wild Rice and Mushrooms *54*

Chicken Pot Pie *56*

Cider-glazed Turkey Breast *57*

Roast Turkey with Dried Cranberry Dressing *58*

Turkey Burgers with Corn Salsa *60*

Roasted Flat Chicken

MAKES 4
TO 6 SERVINGS

I learned how to cook whole chicken flattened under foil-wrapped bricks from Carlo Middione, a great Italian restaurateur in San Francisco, but you can prepare a similar version in the convection oven. Serve with baked beets (page 73) and garlic mashed potatoes.

2 tbsp	Dijon mustard	25 mL
1 tbsp	soy sauce	15 mL
2	cloves garlic, finely chopped	2
2 tsp	chopped fresh rosemary, or ½ tsp (2 mL) dried	10 mL
¼ tsp	black pepper	1 mL
1	3-lb (1.5 kg) chicken, rinsed and patted dry	1

1. In a small bowl, combine mustard, soy sauce, garlic, rosemary and pepper.

2. With kitchen shears or a sharp knife, cut carefully along both sides of backbone. Remove backbone. Cut off wing tips (freeze backbone and wing tips for stock). Spread chicken open and press firmly to flatten.

3. Spoon mustard mixture over both sides of chicken. Arrange chicken, skin side up, on a foil- *and* parchment-lined baking sheet (this will make cleanup easier).

4. Convection roast in a preheated 325°F (160°C) oven for 55 to 60 minutes, or until juices run clear when thigh is pierced or meat thermometer registers 180°F (82°C) when inserted into thigh. If chicken is browning too quickly, cover loosely with foil, tucking edges under chicken, during last half of roasting time. Transfer to a carving board or serving platter and cut into serving pieces.

Crispy Chicken with Cranberry Pear Relish

MAKES 6 SERVINGS

Dipping chicken breasts in the yogurt mixture helps the bread crumbs to cling. Convection oven cooking seals in the juices and produces a crisp exterior and moist, tender chicken. Prepare this lower-fat, flavorful dish to serve with mashed turnips (page 100). The cranberry pear relish can also be served with roast turkey, baked ham and chicken sandwiches.

This recipe also works well with turkey cutlets or flattened pork tenderloin pieces.

CRANBERRY PEAR RELISH

2	pears, peeled, cored and diced	2
1	small onion, chopped	1
1 1/2 cups	fresh or frozen cranberries	375 mL
1 cup	apple juice or orange juice	250 mL
1 tbsp	granulated sugar (optional)	15 mL
2 tbsp	chopped fresh basil or mint	25 mL

CRISPY CHICKEN

3/4 cup	unflavored yogurt or buttermilk	175 mL
1/4 cup	chopped fresh basil, or 2 tsp (10 mL) dried	50 mL
1 tbsp	horseradish	15 mL
2 cups	fresh bread crumbs	500 mL
1/3 cup	grated Parmesan cheese	75 mL
1/4 tsp	salt	1 mL
1/4 tsp	black pepper	1 mL
6	boneless, skinless chicken breasts (about 6 oz/175 g each)	6

1. To prepare relish, in a medium saucepan, combine pears, onion, cranberries, apple juice and sugar, if using. Bring to a boil on high heat. Reduce heat to medium-low and simmer, uncovered, for 15 minutes, or until pears are tender. Stir occasionally. Pour into a bowl and let cool to room temperature. Stir in basil. Cover and refrigerate for up to 3 days.

2. To prepare chicken, combine yogurt, basil and horseradish in a shallow dish. Combine bread crumbs, cheese, salt and pepper in another dish.

3. Pat chicken pieces dry. Dip chicken into yogurt mixture to coat. Roll chicken in bread crumbs, turning to coat and patting in crumbs. Place on a parchment-lined or lightly greased baking sheet.

4. Convection bake in a preheated 350°F (180°C) oven for 25 to 30 minutes, or until juices run clear and chicken is no longer pink inside. Serve with relish.

Roasted Drumsticks and Vegetables

MAKES 5
TO 6 SERVINGS

Weekday family dinners need easy-to-prepare dishes like this one. The chicken and vegetables are cooked together, and you only have to add a crisp salad or a cabbage salad (page 91) for a complete meal.

8	chicken drumsticks	8
2	onions, peeled and quartered	2
6	cloves garlic, peeled	6
4	medium new potatoes, quartered (about 1 ½ lbs/750 g total)	4
4	parsnips, peeled and halved crosswise	4
2	red bell peppers, seeded and cut in eighths	2
2 tbsp	olive oil	25 mL
1 tsp	dried thyme leaves	5 mL
¾ tsp	salt	4 mL
½ tsp	black pepper	2 mL

1. Arrange drumsticks, onions, garlic, potatoes, parsnips and peppers in a single layer on a foil-lined baking sheet.

2. Drizzle oil over chicken and vegetables. Sprinkle with thyme, salt and pepper. Turn to coat.

3. Convection roast in a preheated 325°F (160°C) oven for 60 to 70 minutes, or until vegetables are tender and chicken is golden. Stir twice during cooking time.

Honey Garlic Chicken Wings

MAKES 2
TO 3 SERVINGS

Both kids and adults love these wings. Have moist towelettes on hand for greasy fingers. For a casual gathering serve these along with other finger food such as nachos (page 29) and quesadillas (page 26). If you are not a wing fan, or if you prefer a lower-fat version, use thin boneless, skinless chicken breasts and bake for 20 to 25 minutes, or until the chicken is no longer pink inside. Cover the chicken loosely with foil if it browns too much.

2 lbs	chicken wings	1 kg
¼ cup	liquid honey	50 mL
¼ cup	soy sauce	50 mL
3 tbsp	ketchup	45 mL
2 tbsp	black bean sauce or hoisin sauce	25 mL
2 tbsp	lemon juice or white vinegar	25 mL
3	cloves garlic, minced	3
¼ tsp	ground ginger	1 mL

1. Cut wing tips off chicken (freeze to make stock). Cut each chicken wing into two pieces at the joint.

2. In a large bowl, combine honey, soy sauce, ketchup, black bean sauce, lemon juice, garlic and ginger. Add chicken wings. Stir to coat wings with marinade. Cover and refrigerate for 4 hours or overnight.

3. Arrange chicken wings with marinade on a foil- or parchment-lined baking sheet.

4. Convection bake in a preheated 375°F (190°C) oven for 20 to 25 minutes, turning halfway through cooking.

Stuffed Chicken Breasts with Goat Cheese and Red Pepper Sauce

MAKES 6 SERVINGS

When I teach cooking classes at a bed and breakfast, this recipe is part of a Provençal themed weekend. It is a special dish for entertaining, but requires just a little last-minute cooking. Serve it with Eggplant Olive Tapenade (page 27) and Rosemary Garlic Fougasse (page 138).

Make Ahead
Stuff chicken up to six hours ahead, cover and refrigerate. Red pepper sauce can be prepared, covered and refrigerated up to a day ahead.

RED PEPPER SAUCE

4	red bell peppers	4
¾ cup	chicken stock	175 mL
1 tbsp	olive oil	15 mL
¼ tsp	salt	1 mL
¼ tsp	black pepper	1 mL

STUFFED CHICKEN BREASTS

¾ cup	crumbled goat cheese (about 4 oz/125 g)	175 mL
2 tbsp	olive oil, divided	25 mL
½ tsp	herbes de Provence (page 23) or dried thyme leaves	2 mL
6	boneless, skinless chicken breasts (about 6oz/175 g each)	6
¼ tsp	salt	1 mL
¼ tsp	black pepper	1 mL
⅓ cup	finely shredded fresh basil	75 mL

1. To prepare sauce, arrange red peppers on a baking sheet. Place about 3 inches (7.5 cm) from preheated broiler. Convection broil for 10 to 15 minutes, or until skin is charred, turning peppers about three times during broiling time. Let stand at room temperature until cool enough to handle.

2. Peel peppers and discard seeds and core. (Dip fingers in cold water when peeling peppers to help remove any clinging seeds and skins. Do not rinse peppers.)

3. Cut peppers into large pieces and puree in a food processor or blender until smooth. Add chicken stock, olive oil, salt and pepper. Blend to combine thoroughly. (An immersion blender can also be used.) Refrigerate if not serving immediately. (Just before serving, heat sauce in saucepan.)

4. To prepare chicken, in a small bowl, combine goat cheese, 1 tbsp (15 mL) olive oil and herbes de Provence. Stir until softened.

5. Make a 3-inch (7.5 cm) slit lengthwise in thickest part of chicken breast. Spoon in cheese filling. Close opening with toothpick or skewer. Repeat with remaining chicken breasts. Refrigerate for 1½ hours.

6. Heat remaining 1 tbsp (15 mL) olive oil in a large nonstick skillet over medium-high heat (if you don't have a nonstick skillet, you may need more oil). Sprinkle chicken with salt and pepper. Brown chicken breasts for about 2 minutes per side, or until golden. Place on a parchment-lined baking sheet.

7. Convection bake chicken in a preheated 350°F (180°C) oven for 25 minutes, or until juices run clear and chicken is no longer pink inside. Remove skewers. Serve with sauce. Garnish with shredded basil.

Chicken Souvlaki
with Tzatziki

MAKES 4 SERVINGS

Anyone who has visited Greece and spent leisurely hours in the open-air taverns and restaurants may be transported back with this recipe. Traditionally grilled over charcoal cookers, souvlaki can also be cooked quickly under the broiler. Serve tzatziki as a refreshing side dish or as a spread with warmed pita. Slice fresh tomatoes and lemon wedges to serve alongside, too.

Make Ahead
Tzatziki can be made and refrigerated, covered, up to six hours ahead.

CHICKEN

2 tbsp	olive oil	25 mL
2 tbsp	dry white wine or chicken stock	25 mL
2 tbsp	lemon juice	25 mL
1	clove garlic, minced	1
1 tsp	dried oregano leaves	5 mL
1 tsp	grated lemon zest	5 mL
1/4 tsp	salt	1 mL
1/4 tsp	black pepper	1 mL
3	bay leaves	3
1 lb	boneless, skinless chicken breasts, cut in 1-inch (2.5 cm) pieces	500 g

TZATZIKI

1 cup	unflavored yogurt	250 mL
1/2	English cucumber, grated	1/2
1/2 tsp	salt	2 mL
2	cloves garlic, minced	2
1 tbsp	chopped fresh dillweed	15 mL
1 tbsp	chopped fresh mint	15 mL
1 tbsp	lemon juice	15 mL
	Salt and black pepper to taste	

1. To prepare chicken, combine olive oil, wine, lemon juice, garlic, oregano, lemon zest, salt, pepper, bay leaves and chicken in a large bowl. Stir thoroughly. Cover and refrigerate for 1 to 8 hours.

2. To prepare tzatziki, line a sieve or strainer with cheesecloth or a clean dish towel. Spoon yogurt into sieve. Let drain, refrigerated, for 1 hour.

3. Meanwhile, combine cucumber with salt and place in a strainer. Drain for 30 minutes. Pat cucumber dry.

4. Combine drained yogurt, cucumber, garlic, dill, mint and lemon juice. Taste and season with salt and pepper.

5. To cook souvlaki, thread chicken onto skewers. Arrange on a lightly greased broiler rack. Place 4 inches (10 cm) from heat and convection broil under preheated broiler for 4 minutes. Turn and broil for 4 to 6 minutes longer, or until pinkness disappears. Serve with tzatziki.

Broiled Cilantro Garlic Chicken Breasts

MAKES 4 SERVINGS

This may sound like a lot of garlic and cilantro, but the result is a tangy, moist chicken. In Thailand, I had this served from a hibachi, but it also cooks extremely well in the convection oven. You can also use the marinade on thick slices of extra-firm tofu, but reduce the cooking time by at least half. Serve with sliced tomato and cucumber. This chicken is also good chilled and thinly sliced. Add to a salad with diced mango.

4	boneless, skinless chicken breasts (about 6 oz/175 g each)	4
4	cloves garlic, peeled	4
2	shallots or 1 small onion, peeled	2
1 cup	loosely packed fresh cilantro leaves	250 mL
1/4 cup	lemon juice or lime juice	50 mL
1 tbsp	granulated sugar	15 mL
1 tbsp	fish sauce or soy sauce	15 mL
1 tsp	black pepper	5 mL

1. Place one chicken breast between sheets of parchment paper or plastic wrap (I cut open a plastic bag). With a meat pounder or rolling pin, flatten chicken until about 1/2 inch (1 cm) thick. Place in a shallow glass or ceramic dish. Repeat with remaining chicken breasts.

2. In a food processor or blender, finely chop garlic, shallots and cilantro. Blend in lemon juice, sugar, fish sauce and pepper. Pour over chicken, turning to coat on all sides. Cover and refrigerate for 1 to 12 hours.

3. To cook, arrange chicken breasts with marinade on a lightly greased broiler pan. Place under a preheated broiler about 4 inches (10 cm) from heat. Convection broil for 4 minutes. Turn and broil for 4 to 6 minutes longer, or until chicken is no longer pink inside. Do not overcook or chicken will be dry.

Cornish Hens with Wild Rice and Mushrooms

MAKES 4 SERVINGS

Cornish hens seem to be reserved for special occasions, but these little birds make an easy dinner. As a bonus, they cook in less than an hour. Serve with steamed broccoli to round out the main course.

Dried porcini mushrooms are often found in the produce section in small packages (you may need two packages).

Make Ahead

Wild rice and mushrooms can be transferred to an 8-inch (2 L) square baking dish, covered and refrigerated up to a day ahead. To reheat, cover and convection bake in a preheated 350°F (180°C) oven for 25 minutes, or until hot.

4	Cornish hens (about 1 ¼ lbs/625 g each)	4
½ tsp	dried oregano or thyme leaves	2 mL
½ tsp	salt, divided	2 mL
½ tsp	black pepper, divided	2 mL
1 tbsp	olive oil	15 mL
WILD RICE AND MUSHROOMS		
1 oz	dried porcini mushrooms	30 g
2 tbsp	olive oil or butter	25 mL
1	onion, chopped	1
2	cloves garlic, finely chopped	2
2 cups	sliced fresh mushrooms	500 mL
2½ cups	cooked wild rice	625 mL
1 tbsp	chopped fresh oregano, or 1 tsp (5 mL) dried	15 mL
½ tsp	salt	2 mL
¼ tsp	black pepper	1 mL

1. Pat hens dry. Sprinkle cavities with oregano, ¼ tsp (1 mL) salt and ¼ tsp (1 mL) pepper. Tie legs together. Arrange on a rack over broiler pan. Rub olive oil over hens and sprinkle with remaining ¼ tsp (1 mL) salt and ¼ tsp (1 mL) pepper.

2. Convection roast in a preheated 350°F (180°C) oven for 55 to 60 minutes, or until juices run clear when thigh is pierced. Remove to a platter. Cover loosely with foil and let stand for 10 minutes.

3. While hens are cooking, prepare wild rice and mushrooms. Place dried mushrooms in a bowl. Cover with 1 cup (250 mL) hot water and soak for 20 minutes. Lift out mushrooms, rubbing off any sand. Strain soaking liquid (use cheesecloth, dish towel or coffee filter) and reserve liquid. Chop mushrooms.

4. In a large skillet, heat oil over medium-high heat. Add onion, garlic, fresh mushrooms and $\frac{1}{4}$ cup (50 mL) reserved mushroom liquid. Cook for 6 minutes, stirring occasionally, until mushrooms have softened. Add porcini mushrooms, rice, oregano, salt, pepper and remaining mushroom liquid. Bring just to a boil. Reduce heat to low. Cover and keep warm while hens finish roasting.

Wild Rice

Technically not a rice (it is a seed from an aquatic grass), wild rice is often considered a luxury item, since it is more expensive than other rices. Its dark color, chewy texture and nutty flavor team well with other cooked rices and grains in salads and pilafs.

Cook $\frac{3}{4}$ cup (175 mL) wild rice in plenty of boiling water, uncovered, for 45 minutes, or until rice is tender. Drain well. Makes about $2\frac{1}{2}$ cups (625 mL).

Chicken Pot Pie

MAKES 6 SERVINGS

An all-time favorite. The drop biscuit batter makes a speedy topping. Of course, turkey can also be used or, in a pinch, cooked deli chicken.

3 tbsp	butter	45 mL
1	onion, chopped	1
2	stalks celery, chopped	2
1 cup	diced carrots	250 mL
1 1/2 cups	sliced mushrooms	375 mL
1/4 cup	all-purpose flour	50 mL
2 1/2 cups	chicken stock	625 mL
1/2 tsp	dried thyme leaves	2 mL
1/2 tsp	salt	2 mL
1/2 tsp	black pepper	2 mL
2 1/2 cups	diced cooked chicken	625 mL
1 cup	fresh or frozen peas	250 mL
2 tbsp	chopped fresh parsley	25 mL

TOPPING

1 1/2 cups	all-purpose flour	375 mL
2 tsp	baking powder	10 mL
1/2 tsp	salt	2 mL
1/4 tsp	dried thyme leaves	1 mL
1/3 cup	cold butter, cut in cubes	75 mL
3/4 cup	milk	175 mL
2 tbsp	grated Parmesan cheese	25 mL

1. In a large saucepan, melt butter over medium-high heat. Add onion, celery and carrots. Cook, stirring, for 4 minutes until softened. Add mushrooms and cook for 4 minutes.

2. Add flour and cook, stirring, for 2 minutes. Add stock, thyme, salt and pepper. Bring to a boil and cook for 4 minutes.

3. Stir in chicken, peas and parsley. Heat through. Spoon into a lightly greased 8-cup (2 L) casserole.

4. For the topping, in a large bowl, combine flour, baking powder, salt and thyme. Cut in butter until it is in tiny bits. Add milk, mixing until dough is slightly sticky.

5. Drop batter by spoonfuls over chicken. Sprinkle with Parmesan cheese.

6. Convection bake in a preheated 375°F (190°C) oven for 25 to 30 minutes, or until top is golden and topping is cooked in center.

Cider-glazed Turkey Breast

MAKES 6 TO 8 SERVINGS

For people who like white meat only. For a smaller family this will also provide extra for lunches. Garnish with orange sections and sage leaves.

¼ cup	cider vinegar	50 mL
2 tbsp	coarse-grain mustard	25 mL
2 tbsp	soy sauce	25 mL
2	cloves garlic, finely chopped	2
½ tsp	dried sage or savory leaves	2 mL
½ tsp	salt	2 mL
¼ tsp	black pepper	1 mL
1	3-lb (1.5 kg) turkey breast, bone in	1

1. In a small bowl, whisk together vinegar, mustard, soy sauce, garlic, sage, salt and pepper.
2. Place turkey breast skin side up on a rack over broiler pan. Spread half of vinegar mixture over turkey.
3. Convection roast in a preheated 325°F (160°C) oven for 50 minutes. Baste with vinegar mixture. Continue to roast for 30 to 40 minutes, basting every 15 minutes, until meat thermometer registers 170°F (75°C) when inserted into thickest part. Remove turkey to a platter. Cover loosely with foil and let stand for 10 minutes before carving.

Variation

Mediterranean Glazed Turkey Breast: For the basting mixture, in a small bowl, whisk together 3 tbsp (45 mL) orange juice, 3 tbsp (45 mL) balsamic vinegar, 2 tbsp (25 mL) pesto, 1½ tsp (7 mL) dried thyme leaves, 1 tsp (5 mL) grated orange zest and ½ tsp (2 mL) salt.

Roast Turkey with Dried Cranberry Dressing

MAKES 10 SERVINGS

Turkey with all the trimmings is one of my favorite meals. Often reserved for Thanksgiving or Christmas dinners, I make this off season, even in the summer, and use leftovers in sandwiches and salads.

Many manufacturers recommend not stuffing poultry that is cooked in the convection oven. Whole turkeys and chickens roast more quickly in the convection oven than in a standard oven, sealing in juices and browning the surface. However, in the convection oven the poultry reaches its optimum temperature before the stuffing does, so for safety, the dressing is cooked separately as a side dish.

If your bread crumbs are very fresh, use less stock; use more if the bread is very dry. Day-old French or Italian bread works well.

Start with a fully defrosted bird. If your turkey is frozen, defrost it in the refrigerator. (Be sure to remove the bag of giblets.)

ROAST TURKEY

1	10- to 12-lb (4.5 to 5 kg) turkey	1
8	large sprigs fresh rosemary, divided	8
½ tsp	salt, divided	2 mL
½ tsp	black pepper, divided	2 mL
2	onions, peeled and cut in quarters	2
2 tbsp	olive oil	25 mL

DRIED CRANBERRY AND APRICOT DRESSING

2 tbsp	butter	25 mL
2	onions, chopped	2
3	stalks celery, diced	3
3	cloves garlic, finely chopped	3
8 cups	coarse fresh bread crumbs	2 L
¾ cup	dried cranberries	175 mL
½ cup	diced dried apricots	125 mL
½ cup	toasted chopped pecans (optional)	125 mL
½ cup	chopped fresh parsley	125 mL
2 tbsp	chopped fresh rosemary, or 1½ tsp (7 mL) dried	25 mL
1 tsp	salt	5 mL
½ tsp	black pepper	2 mL
2¾ cups	turkey stock or vegetable stock	675 mL

GRAVY

3 cups	turkey stock (approx.)	750 mL
3 tbsp	butter or turkey drippings	45 mL
¼ cup	all-purpose flour	50 mL
	Salt and black pepper to taste	

1. Remove giblets and neck from turkey. Pat turkey dry inside and out. Loosen breast skin of turkey and tuck in 4 sprigs of rosemary. Season cavity with ¼ tsp (1 mL) salt and ¼ tsp (1 mL) pepper. Place onions and remaining rosemary sprigs in turkey cavity.

2. Place turkey breast side up on a rack over broiler pan. Tuck wing tips under bird. Tie drumsticks together with kitchen string. Brush turkey with olive oil. Sprinkle with remaining ¼ tsp (1 mL) salt and ¼ tsp (1 mL) pepper.

3. Convection roast in a preheated 325°F (160°C) oven for 1¾ to 2¼ hours, or until a meat thermometer inserted into inner thigh registers 180°F (82°C). Remove turkey to a platter. Cover loosely with foil and let stand for 20 minutes before carving.

4. While turkey is cooking, make dressing. In a large skillet, melt butter over medium heat. Add onions, celery and garlic. Cook for 5 minutes, stirring occasionally. Transfer to a large bowl. Add bread crumbs, cranberries, apricots, pecans, if using, parsley, rosemary, salt and pepper. Add stock and combine thoroughly. Turn into a greased 8-cup (2 L) casserole.

5. Bake stuffing, uncovered, with turkey for 1 to 1¼ hours, or until golden brown and hot throughout.

6. To prepare gravy, pour 1 cup (250 mL) stock into the roasting pan. Place on stove over high heat. Scrape bottom to loosen particles and deglaze pan. Strain into a large measuring cup. Add enough stock to make 3 cups (750 mL). Skim fat from surface.

7. In a saucepan, melt butter over medium heat. Add flour and cook, stirring, for 3 minutes, or until golden. Whisk in stock. Bring to a boil. Cook for 6 to 8 minutes, or until slightly thickened. Taste and season with salt and pepper. Serve gravy with carved turkey and dressing.

Turkey Stock
In a large saucepan, combine turkey giblets and neck with 2 peeled onions, 2 carrots and 2 stalks celery (all cut in chunks), 1 bay leaf, ½ tsp (2 mL) dried thyme leaves, ½ tsp (2 mL) whole black peppercorns and 8 cups (2 L) water. Bring to a boil. Reduce heat to low and simmer, uncovered, for 2 hours. Strain and refrigerate. (Stock can be covered and refrigerated for 2 days or frozen for up to 6 weeks.) Makes about 6 cups (1.5 L).

Turkey Burgers with Corn Salsa

MAKES 4 SERVINGS

These burgers can be served with or without the buns. Roast the corn while shaping the burgers, then finish making the salsa while the burgers cook. Serve with Potato and Caesar Salad (page 105). Cold burgers are excellent in sandwiches or salads.

Make Ahead

Shape burgers, cover and refrigerate up to four hours before baking. Make salsa, cover and refrigerate up to six hours ahead.

1 lb	ground turkey	500 g
2	cloves garlic, minced	2
1	green onion, finely chopped	1
1	egg	1
¾ cup	fresh bread crumbs	175 mL
2 tbsp	chili sauce or ketchup	25 mL
1 tbsp	Worcestershire sauce	15 mL
½ tsp	salt	2 mL
½ tsp	black pepper	2 mL
½ tsp	dried savory leaves	2 mL
4	½-inch (1 cm) cubes smoked Gouda or provolone cheese (about 2 oz/60 g)	4

CORN SALSA

1 cup	fresh or frozen corn kernels	250 mL
1 tbsp	olive oil	15 mL
1	tomato, cored and diced	1
1	green onion, finely chopped	1
2 tbsp	chopped fresh cilantro or parsley	25 mL
2 tbsp	lime juice or lemon juice	25 mL
¼ tsp	salt	1 mL
¼ tsp	black pepper	1 mL

1. In a medium bowl, combine turkey, garlic, green onion, egg, bread crumbs, chili sauce, Worcestershire, salt, pepper and savory. Mix thoroughly.

2. With wet hands, divide mixture evenly into four. Make an indentation and tuck a piece of cheese into meat. Form into burgers, enclosing cheese in center. Place burgers on a rack over broiler pan.

3. Convection bake burgers in a preheated 400°F (200°C) oven for 15 to 18 minutes, or until no pinkness remains.

4. Meanwhile, to prepare salsa, toss corn with olive oil in an 8-inch (2 L) square baking dish. Convection bake in preheated 400°F (200°C) oven for 10 minutes, or until starting to turn golden. Stir once during cooking. Let cool for 10 minutes, then combine with tomato, green onion, cilantro, lime juice, salt and pepper. Serve salsa with burgers.

Meat

Roast Prime Rib of Beef *62*

Rib Eye Roast with Beer Mushroom Gravy *63*

Herbed Flank Steak with Polenta *64*

Cheeseburger Pie *66*

Danish Meat Patties *67*

Deep-Dish Tamale Pie *68*

Asian-flavored Meatballs *70*

Baked Ham with Apricot Glaze *71*

Roast Pork Loin with Apples *72*

Crispy Butterflied Pork Chops with Creole Sauce *74*

Glazed Spareribs *76*

Roasted Rack of Lamb *77*

Thyme-scented Leg of Lamb with Beans *78*

Breaded Veal in Tomato Sauce *80*

Roast Prime Rib of Beef

MAKES 6 SERVINGS

For a special and truly delicious meal, few can resist a prime roast beef dinner. Serve with pan juices, potatoes, horseradish and your favorite mustard.

¼ cup	Dijon mustard	50 mL
3	cloves garlic, finely chopped	3
1 tbsp	chopped fresh thyme, or 1 tsp (5 mL) dried	15 mL
1 tbsp	Worcestershire sauce	15 mL
¾ tsp	salt	4 mL
½ tsp	black pepper	2 mL
1	prime rib roast of beef (about 4 lbs/2 kg)	1

SAUCE

1 tbsp	all-purpose flour	15 mL
¾ cup	water	175 mL
½ cup	dry red wine	125 mL
½ tsp	salt	2 mL
¼ tsp	black pepper	1 mL

1. In a small bowl, combine mustard, garlic, thyme, Worcestershire, salt and pepper.

2. Place roast, fat side up, on a rack over broiler pan. Rub paste mixture over top and sides of meat.

3. Convection roast in a preheated 325°F (160°C) oven for 1¾ hours, or until meat is cooked to desired doneness: 140°F (60°C) for rare to medium-rare or 160°F (70°C) for medium. Remove roast to a carving board and cover loosely with foil. Let stand for 10 to 15 minutes before carving.

4. Meanwhile, to prepare sauce, pour fat from roasting pan and place pan on stovetop on medium-high heat. Sprinkle flour over remaining meat juices and cook, stirring, for 2 minutes. Add water and wine. Bring to a boil over medium-high heat, stirring and scraping any caramelized bits from bottom of pan. Reduce heat to medium and cook for 5 minutes. Add any accumulated juices from carving board to sauce. Strain sauce if desired and season with salt and pepper. Serve with sliced roast beef.

Rib Eye Roast with Beer Mushroom Gravy

MAKES 8 TO 10 SERVINGS

Easy-cook roasts and no-fuss sauces make a roast beef dinner a breeze to prepare. Rib eye is a less expensive and less tender roast than prime rib, but it is lean, easy to carve and juicy if not overcooked. Cold leftovers slice easily for meat platters and sandwiches.

1 tsp	dry mustard	5 mL
1 tsp	coarsely ground black pepper	5 mL
1 tsp	Worcestershire sauce	5 mL
1	rib eye roast (about 3½ lbs/1.75 kg)	1

BEER MUSHROOM GRAVY

2 tbsp	butter or olive oil	25 mL
1 lb	mushrooms, sliced	500 g
2 tbsp	all-purpose flour	25 mL
1	12-oz (341 mL) bottle beer or apple juice	1
1 cup	water	250 mL
½ cup	tomato juice or tomato sauce, storebought or homemade (page 80)	125 mL
1	1½-oz (45 g) package dry onion soup mix Salt and black pepper to taste	1

1. In a small bowl, combine mustard, pepper and Worcestershire. Rub over roast. Place roast on a rack over broiler pan.

2. Convection roast in a preheated 350°F (180°C) oven for 1 to 1½ hours, or until internal temperature reaches 140°F (60°C) for rare or 150°F (65°C) for medium-rare. Remove roast to a carving board, cover with foil and let stand for 15 minutes before carving.

3. While meat is roasting, prepare gravy. Heat butter in a large skillet over medium-high heat. Add mushrooms and cook, stirring occasionally, for 8 minutes. Add flour and cook, stirring, for 3 minutes. Add beer, water, tomato juice and onion soup mix. Stir to prevent flour from sticking. Bring to a boil. Reduce heat and simmer for 15 to 20 minutes, or until onions have softened. (Add water or tomato juice if sauce reduces too much.) Season to taste with salt and pepper.

Herbed Flank Steak with Polenta

MAKES 6 SERVINGS

Flank steak, an inexpensive but less tender cut, benefits from overnight marinating. Score the meat to let the robust marinade soak in and help prevent shrinkage.

Chipotle peppers are smoked jalapeño peppers in adobo sauce. They are much hotter than regular jalapeños and are available in cans or jars at specialty food shops and some supermarkets. Freeze any leftover peppers and sauce in small portions.

The polenta, which is made ahead, can be broiled while the flank steak rests. Serve with corn or tomato salsa (pages 60 and 86) and sautéed mushrooms.

Make Ahead
Polenta can be prepared, covered and refrigerated up to a day ahead.

HERBED FLANK STEAK

1	flank steak (about 1 ½ lbs/750 g)	1
4	cloves garlic, finely chopped	4
2 tbsp	Dijon mustard	25 mL
¼ cup	red wine vinegar or sherry vinegar	50 mL
2 tbsp	chopped chipotle peppers with sauce	25 mL
2 tbsp	chopped fresh parsley	25 mL
2 tbsp	chopped fresh cilantro	25 mL
2 tbsp	chopped fresh oregano, or 1 tsp (5 mL) dried	25 mL
¼ cup	olive oil	50 mL

POLENTA

2 cups	milk	500 mL
2 cups	water	500 mL
½ tsp	salt	2 mL
¼ tsp	black pepper	1 mL
1 cup	cornmeal	250 mL
⅓ cup	grated Parmesan cheese	75 mL
2 tsp	chopped fresh oregano, or ½ tsp (2 mL) dried	10 mL
2 tbsp	olive oil	25 mL

1. To prepare meat, score flank steak at an angle several times on each side. Place in a non-metallic dish.

2. In a small bowl, combine garlic, mustard, vinegar, chipotle peppers, parsley, cilantro, oregano and olive oil. Rub into steak. Cover and refrigerate for 6 to 24 hours.

3. To prepare polenta, in a large saucepan, combine milk, water, salt and pepper. Bring to a boil.

4. Gradually add cornmeal while stirring. Reduce heat to medium-low. Cook, stirring, for 12 to 15 minutes, or until very thick.

5. Remove polenta from heat. Stir in Parmesan and oregano.

Asian-flavored Meatballs (page 70)

6. Spread polenta in a greased 9-inch (2.5 L) square baking pan. Cover surface directly with plastic wrap. Cover and refrigerate for 4 to 5 hours, or until cold.

7. Place steak on a rack over broiler pan. Convection broil under a preheated broiler, about 4 inches (10 cm) from heat, for 4 to 6 minutes per side, or until rare. Do not overcook. Remove to a carving board and let stand for 10 minutes before carving thinly on the diagonal.

8. While steak is standing, cut polenta into 9 squares. Brush with olive oil. Place on broiler pan. Broil under preheated broiler for 4 to 6 minutes per side, or until hot and golden. Cut into triangles and serve with steak.

Cilantro

Also known as fresh coriander or Chinese parsley, cilantro is a fresh herb used in Asian, Mexican and Indian cooking. All parts of the herb can be used (some recipes even call for the roots). Wash well and dry in vegetable spinner or towel. Store refrigerated in plastic bags or covered containers.

Fresh parsley can be substituted for those not fond of cilantro's distinctive flavor.

Roast Pork Loin with Apples (page 72)

Cheeseburger Pie

MAKES 6 TO 8
SERVINGS

Cheeseburgers without the bun make an easy weeknight dinner. Most of the condiments are included in the pie, but feel free to serve pickles, tomato slices and lettuce alongside. Any leftover pie makes great sandwiches.

Make Ahead
Pie can be assembled and refrigerated up to four hours before baking.

1 1/2 lbs	lean ground beef	750 g
1 cup	fresh bread crumbs	250 mL
2	eggs	2
1/2 cup	milk	125 mL
1/4 cup	chili sauce	50 mL
1/4 cup	chopped sweet pickle	50 mL
2	green onions, chopped	2
1 tsp	Dijon mustard	5 mL
1/2 tsp	dried oregano leaves	2 mL
3/4 tsp	salt	4 mL
1/4 tsp	black pepper	1 mL
1 1/2 cups	grated Cheddar or Swiss cheese	375 mL

1. In a large bowl, combine ground beef, bread crumbs, eggs, milk, chili sauce, pickle, green onions, mustard, oregano, salt and pepper. Mix thoroughly.

2. Spoon filling into a lightly greased 10-inch (25 cm) pie plate. Convection bake in a preheated 350°F (180°C) oven for 30 minutes.

3. Sprinkle cheese over surface. Continue to bake for 10 minutes. Let stand for 5 minutes. Pour off any fat. Cut into wedges.

Danish Meat Patties

**MAKES 6 SERVINGS
(12 PATTIES)**

Also known as
frikadeller, these
patties resemble mini
meatloaves. Club soda
makes a lighter patty.
The convection oven
cooks these to a crispy
brown without pan-
frying. Serve hot or cold
with pickled beets,
mashed potatoes and
sautéed red cabbage.

8 oz	ground beef	250 g
8 oz	ground veal or pork	250 g
1	onion, finely chopped	1
1 cup	fresh bread crumbs	250 mL
2 tbsp	all-purpose flour	25 mL
1	egg	1
1 tsp	salt	5 mL
1/2 tsp	black pepper	2 mL
1/2 tsp	allspice	2 mL
1 cup	club soda	250 mL
2 tbsp	butter, melted	25 mL
1 tbsp	olive oil	15 mL

1. In a large bowl, combine ground meats, onion,
   bread crumbs, flour, egg, salt, pepper and allspice.
   Mix together well.

2. Beat in club soda until thoroughly incorporated.
   Cover and refrigerate for 1 hour.

3. Using a 1/3 cup (75 mL) measuring cup as a scant
   measure, shape mixture into 12 oval patties. Place on
   a parchment-lined baking sheet.

4. In a small bowl, combine melted butter and oil. Spoon
   over patties. Convection bake or roast in a preheated
   350°F (180°C) oven for 30 to 35 minutes, or until
   patties are brown and starting to crisp.

Deep-Dish Tamale Pie

MAKES 4
TO 5 SERVINGS

Tamales are Mexican snacks of mesa dough wrapped in corn husks, with a sweet or savory filling. This easy-to-prepare dish has some of the tamale flavors, though it is a far cry from the real thing.

Make Ahead

Meat mixture can be prepared and spooned into dish, covered and refrigerated for up to eight hours. Let stand at room temperature for a half hour before adding topping and baking.

MEAT FILLING

2 tbsp	olive oil	25 mL
1	onion, chopped	1
2	cloves garlic, finely chopped	2
1/4 tsp	hot pepper flakes	1 mL
1 lb	lean ground beef	500 g
2 tsp	chili powder	10 mL
1/2 tsp	dried oregano leaves	2 mL
1/4 tsp	ground cumin	1 mL
3/4 tsp	salt	4 mL
1/4 tsp	black pepper	1 mL
1 cup	fresh or frozen corn kernels	250 mL
1 cup	tomato sauce, storebought or homemade (page 80)	250 mL
1/2 cup	chopped stuffed green olives (optional)	125 mL

TOPPING

1 cup	all-purpose flour	250 mL
1/2 cup	cornmeal	125 mL
1 tbsp	baking powder	15 mL
1/2 tsp	salt	2 mL
3/4 cup	grated Cheddar cheese	175 mL
1 cup	buttermilk	250 mL
2 tbsp	vegetable oil	25 mL

1. In a large skillet, heat olive oil over medium-high heat. Add onion, garlic and pepper flakes. Cook, stirring occasionally, for 3 minutes.

2. Add ground beef. Continue to cook, stirring, until pinkness disappears, about 5 minutes.

3. Remove meat from heat. Stir in chili powder, oregano, cumin, salt, pepper, corn, tomato sauce and olives, if using. Spoon into a lightly greased 8-inch (2 L) square baking dish.

4. To prepare topping, in a bowl, combine flour, cornmeal, baking powder, salt and Cheddar.

5. In a small bowl or measuring cup, combine buttermilk and olive oil. Add to dry ingredients. Stir just to combine. Drop batter by spoonful onto top of meat mixture.

6. Convection bake in a preheated 350°F (180°C) oven for 25 to 30 minutes, or until meat mixture is bubbling at edges and biscuit topping is cooked through at center.

Variation

Drop Cheddar Cornmeal Biscuits: Make topping. Drop dough by spoonfuls onto a parchment-lined baking sheet, making 6 to 8 biscuits. Convection bake in a preheated 350°F (180°C) oven for 20 to 25 minutes, or until golden and firm. Makes 6 to 8 biscuits.

Asian-flavored Meatballs

MAKES 4
TO 5 SERVINGS

Oyster sauce, hoisin sauce and plum sauce can be found in most supermarkets. Asian grocery stores will sell several brands of each. Add a spoonful of oyster sauce or hoisin sauce to meatloaf, burgers or stir-fries. (Mushroom vegetarian oyster sauce is also available.)

Serve these meatballs with steamed rice. Garnish with slivered green onions.

Make Ahead

Meatballs can be cooked, covered and refrigerated up to a day ahead or packaged tightly and frozen for up to three weeks.

MEATBALLS

8 oz	ground beef	250 g
8 oz	ground veal or pork	250 g
1/2 cup	fresh bread crumbs	125 mL
1	egg	1
2 tbsp	oyster sauce	25 mL
2	green onions, finely chopped	2
1 tsp	Dijon mustard	5 mL

SAUCE

3/4 cup	pineapple juice	175 mL
1/3 cup	hoisin sauce	75 mL
1/4 cup	plum sauce	50 mL
1/4 cup	rice vinegar	50 mL
1 tbsp	sesame oil	15 mL
2	cloves garlic, minced	2
2 tsp	finely chopped gingerroot	10 mL
1/2 tsp	hot Asian chili sauce (optional)	2 mL

1. In a large bowl, combine ground meats, bread crumbs, egg, oyster sauce, green onions and mustard. With dampened hands, shape into 1-inch (2.5 cm) meatballs. Place on a parchment- or foil-lined baking sheet.

2. Convection bake in a preheated 375°F (190°C) oven for 25 minutes.

3. Meanwhile, to prepare sauce, in a small saucepan, combine pineapple juice, hoisin sauce, plum sauce, vinegar, sesame oil, garlic, ginger and chili sauce, if using. Bring to a boil over medium-high heat. Reduce heat to medium and simmer, stirring occasionally, for 10 minutes, or until slightly thickened.

4. Arrange meatballs in serving dish. Pour sauce over top.

Baked Ham
with Apricot Glaze

MAKES 10 TO 12 SERVINGS

A great glazed ham can share the dinner table with roast turkey at Thanksgiving and Christmas, or it can hold its own as the main meat dish. This juicy ham pairs well with sweet potatoes, turnip and other vegetables. Use leftovers in salads and sandwiches.

Make Ahead
For cold baked hams, bake, cover and refrigerate for up to two days. Any meat will slice more easily when cold, so for cold meat platters, carve after chilling.

1	fully cooked, bone-in smoked ham (about 12 lbs/5.5 kg)	1
2 cups	apricot juice or apple juice	500 mL
½ cup	apricot jam	125 mL
½ cup	packed brown sugar	125 mL
2 tbsp	Dijon mustard	25 mL
2 tbsp	lemon juice or cider vinegar	25 mL
½ tsp	ground ginger	2 mL

1. Trim fat from ham, leaving a layer ¼ inch (5 mm) thick. Cut through fat diagonally to create a crisscross pattern. Place ham in a foil-lined baking pan. Pour juice over ham. Convection bake in a preheated 300°F (150°C) oven for 1½ hours. Baste occasionally, adding water if juice evaporates.

2. In a small bowl, combine jam, sugar, mustard, lemon juice and ginger. Spoon glaze over ham. Continue to bake ham for 30 to 45 minutes, or until meat thermometer registers 140°F (60°C). Baste with glaze every 15 minutes. Transfer ham to a large carving board or serving platter. Cover loosely with foil. Let stand for 15 minutes before carving.

Holiday Dinner for 10
Make the Airplane Snacks and soup ahead (double the recipe for the soup) and reheat the soup just before serving. Make two pumpkin pies ahead of time.

- Airplane Snacks (page 20)
- Roasted Tomato and Garlic Soup (page 32)
- Roast Turkey with Dried Cranberry Dressing (page 58) or Baked Ham with Apricot Glaze (page 71)
- Mashed Potatoes
- Brussels Sprouts with Sauteed Almonds
- Pumpkin Praline Pie (page 160)

Roast Pork Loin with Apples

A succulent roast for family and guests. The apples and onions can cook while the pork is roasting. Serve with baked beets, creamy mashed potatoes and a steamed green vegetable.

Shop for a pork loin roast with the bones Frenched (trimmed to expose the bones) and the back bone removed for easy carving.

PORK LOIN

1 tsp	dry mustard	5 mL
½ tsp	curry powder	2 mL
½ tsp	salt	2 mL
¼ tsp	black pepper	1 mL
¼ tsp	ground ginger	1 mL
1	pork loin rib roast (about 4 lbs/2 kg)	1
15	sprigs rosemary, 1 inch (2.5 cm) long	15
⅓ cup	marmalade	75 mL
¼ cup	orange juice	50 mL
2 tbsp	Dijon mustard	25 mL

APPLES AND ONIONS

5	apples, peeled, cored and quartered	5
2	onions, cut in wedges	2
2 tbsp	olive oil	25 mL
1 tbsp	fresh rosemary leaves	15 mL
¼ tsp	salt	1 mL
¼ tsp	black pepper	1 mL

1. In a small bowl, combine dry mustard, curry powder, salt, pepper and ginger. Rub mixture into roast.

2. With tip of a sharp knife, pierce roast in several places and insert rosemary sprigs. Place roast rib side down on a rack set over broiler pan.

3. Convection roast in a preheated 325°F (160°C) oven for 1¾ to 2 hours, or until meat thermometer registers 160°F (70°C) to 170°F (75°C).

4. For glaze, in a small bowl, combine marmalade, orange juice and Dijon mustard. Spoon over roast at intervals during the last 45 minutes of cooking time.

5. Meanwhile, in a large bowl, toss apples and onions with olive oil, rosemary, salt and pepper. Place in a shallow baking dish. Roast with pork for 45 to 50 minutes, or until apples are tender.

6. Transfer roast to a carving board. Cover loosely with foil and let stand for 15 minutes before carving. Spoon apples and onions around carved roast. Spoon accumulated juices over meat.

Baked Beets

Place 1½ lbs (750 g) trimmed, unpeeled beets (about 7 medium) on a large sheet of heavy foil. Drizzle beets with 1 tbsp (15 mL) olive oil. Wrap beets tightly in foil, place on a baking sheet and convection bake or roast at 325°F (160°C) for 1½ hours, or until tender. When cool enough to handle, peel beets, cut into slices and place in a large bowl.

In a small bowl, combine 1 tbsp (15 mL) olive oil, 2 tbsp (25 mL) orange juice, 2 tbsp (25 mL) chopped fresh dillweed, ½ tsp (2 mL) salt and ¼ tsp (1 mL) black pepper. Toss beets with dressing. Serve warm or at room temperature. Makes 6 servings.

Crispy Butterflied Pork Chops with Creole Sauce

MAKES 6 SERVINGS

The protective coating of seasoned crumbs adds flavor and crispness to these chops. Bread the meat just before cooking and make the sauce while the chops cook.

Serve with baked sweet potatoes. Start the sweet potatoes in the oven ahead of the pork. If the potatoes are cooked before the pork, remove and let stand for up to 10 minutes. They retain heat well.

The sauce also goes well with chicken or ham.

Make Ahead
The sauce can be made, covered and refrigerated up to two days ahead.

PORK CHOPS

1 cup	corn flakes cereal crumbs	250 mL
1 cup	dry bread crumbs	250 mL
½ tsp	dried thyme leaves	2 mL
½ tsp	dried oregano leaves	2 mL
½ tsp	garlic powder	2 mL
½ tsp	paprika	2 mL
½ tsp	salt	2 mL
½ tsp	black pepper	2 mL
¼ tsp	cayenne pepper	1 mL
½ cup	buttermilk or unflavored yogurt	125 mL
6	butterflied pork chops (about 6 oz/175 g each)	6

CREOLE SAUCE

2 tbsp	olive oil	25 mL
1	onion, chopped	1
2	cloves garlic, finely chopped	2
1	stalk celery, chopped	1
1	red bell pepper, seeded and chopped	1
1	28-oz (796 mL) can plum tomatoes, with juices, chopped	1
¼ tsp	dried oregano leaves	1 mL
¼ tsp	dried thyme leaves	1 mL
¼ tsp	hot pepper sauce	1 mL
¼ tsp	salt	1 mL
¼ tsp	black pepper	1 mL
2 tbsp	chopped fresh parsley	25 mL

1. In a shallow dish, combine corn flakes, bread crumbs, thyme, oregano, garlic powder, paprika, salt, pepper and cayenne. Pour buttermilk into a separate shallow dish.

2. Trim fat from pork chops. Dip chops in buttermilk on both sides, shaking off excess. Place chops in crumb mixture, turning and pressing in crumbs.

3. Arrange chops on a lightly greased rack set over broiler pan. Convection bake in a preheated 325°F (160°C) oven for 35 minutes, or until juices run clear and meat is no longer pink.

4. Meanwhile, to prepare sauce, heat oil in a medium saucepan over medium-high heat. Add onion, garlic, celery and red pepper. Cook, stirring occasionally, for 5 minutes.

5. Add tomatoes, oregano and thyme. Cook over medium-low heat for 25 minutes.

6. Add hot pepper sauce, salt and pepper. Taste and adjust seasonings if necessary. Stir in parsley.

Baked Sweet Potatoes
Pierce 6 medium sweet potatoes with a fork. Place on a baking sheet. Convection bake in a preheated 325°F (160°C) oven for 1 to 1¼ hours, or until tender when tested with a skewer. Makes 6 servings.

Glazed Spareribs

MAKES 3
TO 4 SERVINGS

Serve these with baked beans (page 87) and a cabbage salad (page 91).

2 tbsp	packed brown sugar	25 mL
1 tsp	dried oregano leaves	5 mL
1 tsp	chili powder	5 mL
1 tsp	dry mustard	5 mL
1/2 tsp	ground cumin	2 mL
1/2 tsp	ground cinnamon	2 mL
4 lbs	pork spareribs (back or side)	2 kg
1 cup	barbecue sauce, storebought or homemade	250 mL

1. In a small bowl, combine sugar, oregano, chili powder, mustard, cumin and cinnamon.

2. Place ribs in a large flat dish. Rub seasoning mixture into both sides of ribs. Cover and refrigerate for 4 to 24 hours.

3. Arrange ribs on a rack over broiler pan. Convection roast in a preheated 300°F (150°C) oven for $1\frac{1}{2}$ to $1\frac{3}{4}$ hours, or until meat is tender when pierced with tip of a sharp knife. Brush with sauce during last 45 minutes. Cut ribs into serving-size pieces.

Barbecue Sauce

In a large saucepan, heat 2 tbsp (25 mL) olive oil over medium heat. Add 2 finely chopped onions and 6 finely chopped cloves garlic. Cook for 4 minutes until softened. Add $1\frac{1}{2}$ cups (375 mL) tomato sauce, $\frac{3}{4}$ cup (175 mL) water, $\frac{1}{3}$ cup (75 mL) cider vinegar, $\frac{1}{3}$ cup (75 mL) hoisin sauce, $\frac{1}{4}$ cup (50 mL) liquid honey, 2 tbsp (25 mL) Worcestershire sauce, 2 tbsp (25 mL) Dijon mustard, 1 tsp (5 mL) ground cumin and 1 tsp (5 mL) dried oregano leaves. Simmer, stirring occasionally, for 30 to 35 minutes, or until thickened.

Sauce can be refrigerated for three days or frozen for six weeks. Makes about 5 cups (1.25 L).

Roasted Rack of Lamb

MAKES 4 SERVINGS

For several years, I assisted Jacques Pépin when he taught at Bonnie Stern's School of Cooking. Always inspired, I would cook intensely for weeks after his classes. This is an adaptation of a quick recipe that he assembled after a class trip to the market. Although he made it with lamb loins, rack of lamb also works well. Use the marinade for chicken, turkey or pork tenderloin. Serve with roasted asparagus.

1/3 cup	tightly packed fresh mint leaves	75 mL
1/2	jalapeño pepper, seeded	1/2
1 tbsp	coarsely chopped gingerroot	15 mL
2	cloves garlic, peeled	2
2 tbsp	apricot jam	25 mL
1 tbsp	soy sauce	15 mL
2	Frenched racks of lamb, about 8 bones each (1 1/4 lbs/625 g total)	2

1. In a food processor, combine mint, jalapeño, ginger, garlic, jam and soy sauce. Puree until smooth to make a paste.

2. Pat lamb dry. Spread paste over lamb. Cover and refrigerate for 3 hours.

3. Place rack over broiler pan. Preheat pan and rack in a 400°F (200°C) oven on convection roast setting. When oven is preheated place lamb on rack, bone side down. Return to oven and roast for 10 minutes. Reduce temperature to 350°F (180°C). Continue to roast for 15 minutes, or until internal temperature reaches 140°F (60°C) for medium-rare. Remove lamb to a carving board. Cover with foil and let stand for 10 minutes before carving.

Roasted Asparagus
Toss 1 lb (500 g) trimmed asparagus (fat stalks work best) with 1 tbsp (15 mL) olive oil, 1/4 tsp (1 mL) salt and 1/4 tsp (1 mL) black pepper. Place on a parchment-lined baking sheet. Convection roast or bake in a preheated 350°F (180°C) oven for 12 minutes, or until just tender. Turn once during cooking. Makes 4 servings.

Thyme-scented
Leg of Lamb with Beans

MAKES 8 SERVINGS

Roasted leg of lamb
is a special company
meal. Slightly perfumed
with fresh thyme and
garlic slivers, this is
excellent served as a
plain roast. The bean
and vegetable stew
can be served as an
accompaniment or
as a main course for
vegetarian guests.

Make Ahead
Beans can be assembled,
covered and refrigerated
up to six hours ahead.
Let stand at room
temperature for 30
minutes before baking.

1	4- to 5-lb (2 to 2.5 kg) leg of lamb, trimmed	1
2 tsp	olive oil	10 mL
3	cloves garlic, slivered	3
8	sprigs fresh thyme	8
½ tsp	salt	2 mL
¼ tsp	black pepper	1 mL
BEAN STEW		
2 tbsp	olive oil	25 mL
2	onions, thinly sliced	2
4	cloves garlic, slivered	4
2	medium zucchini (about 8 oz/250 g each), halved and cut in ¼-inch (5 mm) slices	2
1	28-oz (796 mL) can plum tomatoes, drained (reserving ¼ cup/50 mL juices) and chopped	1
1	19-oz (540 mL) can Romano beans, drained and rinsed	1
½ tsp	dried marjoram or savory leaves	2 mL
½ tsp	salt	2 mL
¼ tsp	black pepper	1 mL

1. With tip of a sharp knife, pierce lamb in several places. Rub with olive oil. Insert garlic slivers and thyme sprigs. Sprinkle with salt and pepper. Place on a rack over broiler pan.

2. Convection roast in a preheated 325°F (160°C) oven for 1¼ to 1½ hours, or until meat thermometer registers 140°F (60°C) for rare. Remove to a carving board and cover loosely with foil. Let stand for 15 minutes before carving.

3. While lamb is roasting, prepare beans. Heat oil in a large skillet over medium-high heat. Add onions and garlic. Cook, stirring occasionally, for 5 minutes, until onions start to turn golden.

4. Add zucchini and cook, stirring occasionally, for 6 minutes.

5. Stir in tomatoes and reserved juices, beans, marjoram, salt and pepper. Bring to a boil. Transfer to a lightly greased 8-cup (2 L) baking dish.

6. Convection roast beans with lamb for 30 minutes, or until bubbling. (Beans will keep warm for 20 minutes if covered with foil after removing from oven.) Serve beans with carved lamb.

Provençal Dinner for 6

Make the fougasse, shortbread and tapenade ahead of time. Cook the lamb and peppers in the oven at the same time.

- Eggplant Olive Tapenade (page 27)
- Thyme-scented Leg of Lamb with Beans (page 78)
- Summer Peppers (page 98)
- Rosemary Garlic Fougasse (page 138)
- Lavender Shortbread (page 141)

Breaded Veal in Tomato Sauce

MAKES 5 TO 6 SERVINGS

There are as many variations of this dish as there are cooks. Sometimes the breading mixtures contain grated Parmesan; mozzarella slices and basil leaves may also be added during the last ten minutes. Thin pork cutlets, chicken and turkey work well in this recipe, too. Serve it with a simple salad.

Make Ahead

Tomato sauce can be prepared, covered and refrigerated two days in advance.

Scallopini can be breaded, covered and refrigerated four hours before cooking.

TOMATO SAUCE

2 tbsp	olive oil	25 mL
2	onions, chopped	2
2	cloves garlic, finely chopped	2
Pinch	hot pepper flakes	Pinch
½ cup	dry white wine	125 mL
2	28-oz (796 mL) cans plum tomatoes, pureed with juices	2
1 tsp	dried sage leaves	5 mL
¾ tsp	salt	4 mL
¼ tsp	black pepper	1 mL

BREADED VEAL

1 lb	veal scallopini	500 g
½ cup	all-purpose flour	125 mL
3	eggs, beaten	3
2½ cups	fine fresh bread crumbs	625 mL
¼ cup	vegetable oil or olive oil (approx.)	50 mL

1. To prepare sauce, heat oil in a large skillet over medium heat. Add onions, garlic and pepper flakes. Cook, stirring occasionally, for 4 minutes. Add wine and cook for 3 minutes. Add tomatoes, sage, salt and pepper. Cook for 25 minutes, or until sauce thickens. Stir frequently.

2. Meanwhile, to prepare veal, pat pieces dry. Place flour, eggs and bread crumbs in three separate shallow dishes. Dip veal into flour, then into egg and finally into bread crumbs, patting in on both sides. Place veal on wax paper-lined tray.

3. In a large skillet, heat 2 tbsp (25 mL) oil over medium-high heat. Cook veal in batches for about 30 seconds per side, or until golden. Add oil as required.

4. Spoon half of tomato sauce into a 13- by 9-inch (3 L) baking dish (or use 2 smaller dishes). Arrange scallopini on sauce, overlapping slightly. Pour remaining tomato sauce over veal.

5. Convection bake in a preheated 350°F (180°C) oven for 25 to 30 minutes, or until sauce is bubbling.

One-Dish Suppers

Cabbage Roll Bake *82*

Risotto with Sausages and Tomatoes *83*

Tortellini Casserole *84*

Baked Spaghetti Carbonara *85*

Santa Fe Chicken Wraps *86*

Speedy Baked Beans *87*

Eggplant with Mozzarella and Tomato Sauce *88*

Turkey Shepherd's Pie *89*

Tourtière *90*

Chicken and Spinach Pie *92*

Chickpea and Vegetable Curry *94*

Cabbage Roll Bake

MAKES 6 SERVINGS

Enjoy cabbage roll flavors without the fuss of making individual rolls. This is also a great dish to make if you have a lot of leftover cooked rice.

Make Ahead

Assemble dish. Cover and refrigerate up to six hours ahead. Bring to room temperature before baking.

4 cups	shredded cabbage	1 L
2 tbsp	olive oil	25 mL
2	onions, chopped	2
2	cloves garlic, chopped	2
12 oz	lean ground beef	375 g
8 oz	mushrooms, sliced	250 g
2 cups	tomato sauce, storebought or homemade (page 80)	500 mL
2 cups	cooked white rice	500 mL
1 tsp	salt	5 mL
1/2 tsp	black pepper	2 mL
1/2 tsp	dried savory or marjoram leaves	2 mL

1. Bring a large pot of salted water to a boil. Add cabbage and cook for 5 minutes. Drain well.

2. Meanwhile, heat oil in a large skillet over medium-high heat. Add onions and garlic and cook, stirring occasionally, for 3 minutes. Add beef and cook, stirring, until pinkness disappears, about 4 minutes. Add mushrooms and cook for 4 minutes, or until moisture evaporates.

3. Stir in cabbage, tomato sauce, rice, salt, pepper and savory. Mix thoroughly and turn into a lightly greased 13- by 9-inch (3 L) baking dish.

4. Convection bake in a preheated 350°F (180°C) oven for 30 minutes, or until hot in center and bubbling at edges.

Risotto with Sausages and Tomatoes

Traditionally, risotto is cooked on the stovetop, and it involves almost constant stirring. This oven version eliminates all that stirring, allowing you time to prepare an accompanying salad to complete the meal.

Smoked paprika is available in some specialty food shops. If you can find it, use it to replace the regular paprika. Make this dish in a large ovenproof skillet, and serve the risotto directly from the pan.

1 tbsp	olive oil	15 mL
1 lb	sweet Italian sausages (about 4), cut in 1-inch (2.5 cm) pieces	500 g
5	tomatoes, divided	5
2	onions, chopped	2
3	cloves garlic, coarsely chopped	3
1 cup	uncooked arborio rice	250 mL
3 cups	chicken stock	750 mL
1/3 cup	dry sherry or white wine	75 mL
2 tsp	paprika	10 mL
1/2 tsp	ground cumin	2 mL
1/2 tsp	salt	2 mL
1/2 tsp	black pepper	2 mL
1/4 cup	chopped fresh parsley	50 mL

1. In a large ovenproof skillet, heat oil over medium-high heat. Add sausages and cook for 5 to 7 minutes, stirring occasionally. Pour off all but 2 tbsp (25 mL) fat.

2. Core and dice 2 tomatoes. Add onions, garlic and diced tomatoes to skillet. Cook for 4 minutes or until softened.

3. Add rice, stock, sherry, paprika, cumin, salt and pepper. Bring mixture to a boil.

4. Core remaining 3 tomatoes and cut in wedges. Place tomato wedges on top of rice.

5. Transfer skillet to oven and convection bake, uncovered, in a preheated 350°F (180°C) oven for 45 minutes, or until rice is tender.

6. Remove skillet from oven. Cover and let stand for 15 minutes. Sprinkle rice with parsley before serving.

Tortellini Casserole

Pasta dishes cooked in gratins and shallow baking dishes utilize the circulating air of the convection oven, resulting in a golden, crusty surface.

Here a creamy tomato sauce is combined with cheese and tortellini for an easy supper dish. Several kinds of tortellini are available in the frozen food section, so choose your family's favorite.

3 tbsp	butter	45 mL
1	onion, chopped	1
2	cloves garlic, finely chopped	2
3 tbsp	all-purpose flour	45 mL
2 cups	hot milk	500 mL
1 cup	tomato sauce, storebought or homemade (page 80)	250 mL
2 tsp	chopped fresh oregano, or ½ tsp (2 mL) dried	10 mL
¾ tsp	salt	4 mL
½ tsp	black pepper	2 mL
1 lb	frozen cheese or meat tortellini	500 g
1½ cups	grated Cheddar cheese	375 mL
¼ cup	grated Parmesan cheese	50 mL

1. In a medium saucepan, melt butter over medium heat. Add onion and garlic and cook for 3 minutes, stirring occasionally, until softened. Stir in flour. Cook for 3 minutes, stirring, but do not brown.

2. Whisk in hot milk and bring to a boil. Add tomato sauce, oregano, salt and pepper. Cook, stirring often, for 3 minutes.

3. Meanwhile, bring a large pot of salted water to a boil. Add frozen tortellini and cook for 7 to 8 minutes, or until just tender. Drain well.

4. Combine tortellini with Cheddar and sauce. Pour into a lightly greased 8-cup (2 L) shallow baking dish. Sprinkle with Parmesan cheese.

5. Convection bake in a preheated 325°F (160°C) oven for 25 minutes, or until bubbling and lightly browned.

Baked Spaghetti Carbonara

MAKES 5 SERVINGS

This favorite pasta dish bakes quickly in the convection oven. It is an ideal dish for a brunch buffet.

Make Ahead
Assemble dish completely. Cover and refrigerate up to four hours ahead. Bake for an additional five minutes, or until set.

1 lb	uncooked spaghetti	500 g
6	slices bacon, diced	6
1	onion, chopped	1
4	eggs	4
1 cup	light (5%) cream	250 mL
1 cup	milk	250 mL
1/2 cup	grated Parmesan cheese	125 mL
1/4 cup	chopped fresh parsley	50 mL
1/4 tsp	salt	1 mL
1/4 tsp	black pepper	1 mL

1. Break spaghetti in half. Bring a large pot of salted water to a boil. Add spaghetti and cook until just tender, about 10 minutes. Drain well.

2. Meanwhile, cook bacon in a small skillet over medium-high heat until almost crispy, about 4 minutes. Drain off all but 1 tbsp (15 mL) fat.

3. Add onion and cook for 2 minutes until softened.

4. In a large bowl, beat eggs. Add cream, milk, cheese, parsley, salt and pepper. Stir in spaghetti, bacon and onion.

5. Pour into a lightly greased 8-cup (2 L) shallow baking dish. Convection bake in a preheated 325°F (160°C) oven for 22 to 25 minutes, or until set.

Santa Fe Chicken Wraps

MAKES 4
TO 6 SERVINGS

Use leftover turkey or chicken or cooked deli chicken or diced ham in this recipe. Choose mild, medium or hot bottled salsa according to your family's tastes. Serve with fresh homemade salsa, if desired.

Make Ahead
The wraps can be assembled, covered and refrigerated up to six hours ahead. Let stand at room temperature for a half hour before cooking.

3 cups	diced cooked chicken	750 mL
1	green bell pepper, seeded and diced	1
2	green onions, chopped	2
1 tsp	dried oregano leaves	5 mL
1½ cups	grated Monterey Jack or Cheddar cheese, divided	375 mL
3½ cups	salsa, divided	875 mL
8	6-inch (15 cm) flour tortillas	8

1. In a bowl, combine chicken, green pepper, green onions, oregano, ¾ cup (175 mL) cheese and 1 cup (250 mL) salsa. Mix thoroughly.

2. Arrange tortillas on a flat surface. Spread filling evenly over tortillas. Roll up tortillas.

3. Spoon 1 cup (250 mL) salsa in bottom of a lightly greased 13- by 9-inch (3 L) baking dish. Place tortillas on salsa, seam side down. Spoon remaining 1½ cups (375 mL) salsa over tortillas. Sprinkle with remaining ¾ cup (175 mL) cheese.

4. Convection bake, uncovered, in a preheated 350°C (180°C) oven for 20 to 25 minutes, or until hot and bubbling.

Variation
Santa Fe Tofu Wraps: Replace chicken with 3 cups (750 mL) diced extra-firm tofu.

Fresh Tomato Salsa
In a medium bowl, combine 2 cored and diced tomatoes, 1 peeled and diced avocado, 1 chopped green onion, 1 tbsp (15 mL) chopped jalapeño pepper, 2 tbsp (25 mL) chopped fresh cilantro, 3 tbsp (45 mL) lime juice or lemon juice, ¼ tsp (1 mL) salt and ¼ tsp (1 mL) black pepper. Makes about 1¾ cups (425 mL).

Speedy Baked Beans

MAKES 3
TO 4 SERVINGS

For baked bean lovers, this is a quick dish that can be made with ingredients in your pantry. Try different kinds of beans such as black beans, black-eyed peas or aduki beans. For a larger group, double or triple the recipe.

You can also add up to 1 cup (250 mL) diced ham, cooked sausage or bacon to the beans. Serve with Oven Home Fries with Peameal Bacon (page 120), Summer Peppers (page 98) and a chopped vegetable salad.

1 tbsp	olive oil	15 mL
1	onion, chopped	1
¾ cup	tomato sauce, storebought or homemade (page 80)	175 mL
¼ cup	diced sun-dried tomatoes (dry or oil-packed)	50 mL
3 tbsp	maple syrup or brown sugar	45 mL
1 tbsp	Dijon mustard	15 mL
2 tsp	Worcestershire sauce	10 mL
1 tsp	dried oregano leaves	5 mL
1	19-oz (540 mL) can Romano or white beans, drained and rinsed	1
½ tsp	salt	2 mL
½ tsp	black pepper	2 mL

1. In a small skillet, heat oil over medium-high heat. Add onion and cook for 3 minutes, stirring occasionally, until softened.

2. In a large bowl, combine onion, tomato sauce, sun-dried tomatoes, maple syrup, mustard, Worcestershire, oregano, beans, salt and pepper. Mix thoroughly. Spoon into a lightly greased 6-cup (1.5 L) casserole.

3. Convection bake, covered, in a preheated 375°F (190°C) oven for 15 minutes. Uncover and bake for 15 minutes longer, or until hot and bubbling.

Eggplant with Mozzarella and Tomato Sauce

MAKES 4
TO 5 SERVINGS

Buy firm, shiny eggplants that feel weighty in the hand. Eggplants absorb oil like a sponge, so brush sparingly.

Make Ahead

Cook up to three hours ahead and serve at room temperature. The dish can also be assembled ahead, covered and refrigerated overnight. Let stand at room temperature for a half hour before baking. (You may need to bake for an additional five minutes to heat through completely.)

2	large eggplants (about 1 1/4 lbs/625 g each)	2
3 tbsp	olive oil, divided	45 mL
1/4 tsp	salt	1 mL
1/4 tsp	black pepper	1 mL
2 cups	tomato sauce, storebought or homemade (page 80)	500 mL
1 cup	grated mozzarella cheese	250 mL
12	fresh basil leaves	12
1/3 cup	grated Parmesan cheese	75 mL

1. Cut eggplants crosswise into 1/2-inch (1 cm) slices. Arrange in a single layer on lightly greased baking sheets. Brush with half the olive oil. Place about 4 inches (10 cm) from heat and convection broil under preheated broiler until golden, about 6 minutes. Sprinkle with salt and pepper. Turn slices over. Brush with remaining olive oil. Broil for 6 minutes on second side.

2. Spoon 1 cup (250 mL) tomato sauce over bottom of a lightly greased 13- by 9-inch (3 L) baking dish. Arrange eggplant slices over sauce, overlapping as necessary. Sprinkle mozzarella over eggplant. Arrange basil leaves over mozzarella. Spoon over remaining tomato sauce. Sprinkle with Parmesan.

3. Convection bake in a preheated 350°F (180°C) oven for 20 minutes, or until sauce is bubbling and eggplant is hot. Remove from oven and let stand for 5 minutes before serving.

Roasted Eggplant Salad

Roast eggplant slices and arrange on a serving platter. Drizzle with 2 tbsp (25 mL) lemon juice, 2 tbsp (25 mL) chopped fresh parsley and 2 tsp (10 mL) chopped fresh oregano. Makes 4 to 5 servings.

Turkey Shepherd's Pie

MAKES 8 SERVINGS

In this recipe, ground turkey serves as a replacement for the traditional ground beef, though lean ground beef could also be used. Use Yukon Gold or an all-purpose potato that mashes well. You could also use sweet potatoes instead of all or some of the potatoes.

Make Ahead
The dish can be assembled, covered and refrigerated overnight. Let stand at room temperature for a half hour before cooking.

2 lbs	potatoes (about 4 medium), peeled and cut in 1-inch (2.5 cm) pieces	1 kg
½ cup	milk	125 mL
4 tbsp	butter, divided	50 mL
¾ tsp	salt	4 mL
½ tsp	black pepper, divided	2 mL
1	green onion, chopped	1
2 tbsp	chopped fresh parsley	25 mL
1	onion, chopped	1
2	stalks celery, diced	2
8 oz	mushrooms, sliced	250 g
½ cup	diced red bell pepper (optional)	125 mL
1½ lbs	ground turkey	750 g
2 tbsp	all-purpose flour	25 mL
1 cup	chicken stock	250 mL
3 tbsp	soy sauce	45 mL
½ tsp	dried thyme or savory leaves	2 mL
2 cups	fresh or frozen peas	500 mL

1. In a large saucepan, cover potatoes with salted water and bring to a boil. Boil for about 20 minutes, or until tender. Drain well. Mash potatoes with milk, 2 tbsp (25 mL) butter, salt, ¼ tsp (1 mL) pepper, green onion and parsley.

2. Meanwhile, in a large skillet, melt remaining 2 tbsp (25 mL) butter over medium-high heat. Add onion and celery. Cook, stirring occasionally, for 4 minutes. Add mushrooms and red pepper, if using. Cook, stirring occasionally, for 4 minutes. Add turkey and cook, stirring, until all pinkness disappears, about 4 minutes.

3. Stir in flour and cook, stirring, for 2 minutes. Add stock, soy sauce, thyme and remaining ¼ tsp (1 mL) pepper. Cook for 4 minutes, stirring, until mixture thickens. Stir in peas.

4. Spoon turkey mixture into a lightly greased 10-cup (2.5 L) shallow baking dish. Spread potato mixture over meat.

5. Convection bake in a preheated 350°F (180°C) oven for 35 minutes, or until sauce is bubbling around outside and top is golden brown.

Tourtière

MAKES 6 SERVINGS

Tourtière is a tradition in many households during the holiday season. Serve with baked beans (page 87), cabbage salad, chili sauce or ketchup.

Make Ahead

The filling can be prepared, covered and refrigerated up to a day ahead. To freeze the pie unbaked, wrap well and freeze for up to one month. Defrost in the refrigerator for 24 hours, then bake. To freeze baked, wrap well and freeze for up to two weeks. Defrost in the refrigerator for 24 hours. Reheat at 275°F (140°C) for up to 45 minutes, or until hot in the center.

FILLING

2 tbsp	olive oil	25 mL
1	onion, chopped	1
2	cloves garlic, finely chopped	2
½ cup	chopped celery	125 mL
1½ lbs	ground pork, beef, veal or chicken	750 g
1 cup	peeled and grated raw potato	250 mL
½ cup	water	125 mL
2 tbsp	chopped fresh parsley	25 mL
1 tsp	salt	5 mL
½ tsp	dried savory leaves	2 mL
½ tsp	dried thyme leaves	2 mL
¼ tsp	black pepper	1 mL
Pinch	ground cloves	Pinch
Pinch	ground cinnamon	Pinch

PASTRY

1	double recipe All-Purpose Pastry (page 160)	1

GLAZE

1	egg	1
2 tsp	milk	10 mL

1. To prepare filling, heat oil in a large skillet over medium-high heat. Add onion, garlic and celery. Cook, stirring occasionally, for 3 minutes.

2. Add meat to skillet and cook, stirring, for about 8 minutes, or until all traces of pink disappear.

3. Add potato, water, parsley, salt, savory, thyme, pepper, cloves and cinnamon. Reduce heat to low. Cover and simmer for 30 minutes, stirring occasionally. Taste and adjust seasonings if necessary.

4. Spoon filling into a bowl. Cover and refrigerate until cold (adding hot filling to pie shell will make pastry soggy).

5. Divide pastry into two pieces, one piece slightly larger than the other. Roll out larger piece on a lightly floured surface and fit into a 10-inch (25 cm) pie plate with edges overhanging about 1 inch (2.5 cm). Spoon in filling. Roll out remaining pastry and place over filling. Seal pastry edges, trim and flute edges. Cut steam vents in upper crust.

6. In a small bowl, combine egg and milk. Brush over top of pastry. Convection bake or roast in a preheated 375°F (190°C) oven for 40 to 45 minutes, or until pastry is golden.

Cabbage and Apple Salad
In a large bowl, combine 4 cups (1 L) shredded cabbage, 3 chopped green onions, 1 grated carrot, 2 diced red apples and ¼ cup (50 mL) chopped parsley. In a small bowl, stir together ⅓ cup (75 mL) mayonnaise, ⅓ cup (75 mL) sour cream or unflavored yogurt, 1 tbsp (15 mL) lemon juice, 1 tbsp (15 mL) mango chutney, ½ tsp (2 mL) salt and ¼ tsp (1 mL) curry powder. Toss cabbage mixture with dressing and combine well. Makes 6 servings.

Chicken and Spinach Pie

MAKES 6
TO 8 SERVINGS

Pitta, as it is known
in Greek cooking,
is a savory pie filled
with the choices of the
cook. Traditionally it is
made with homemade
phyllo, but fortunately
good-quality phyllo is
available in the frozen
food section. Fillings
vary from cheese and
spinach to chicken and
fennel, and I have also
used finely diced ham
or turkey. Although the
assembly takes some
time, the result is worth
the effort.

For a vegetarian
version, use 1 lb (500 g)
finely chopped extra-firm
tofu instead of chicken.
You could also use
crumbled feta instead of
ricotta, but take care not
to oversalt the filling.

Make Ahead

Filling can be cooked,
covered and refrigerated
up to six hours ahead. Pie
can be assembled, covered
and refrigerated up to an
hour before baking.

FILLING

2 tbsp	olive oil	25 mL
2	onions, chopped	2
3	green onions, chopped	3
1/4 cup	chopped fresh parsley	50 mL
1/4 cup	chopped fresh dillweed	50 mL
2 tbsp	chopped fresh mint	25 mL
1 lb	smoked chicken, finely chopped	500 g
1	10-oz (300 g) package chopped frozen spinach, defrosted and squeezed dry	1
1 cup	ricotta cheese	250 mL
2	eggs, beaten	2
1/4 tsp	salt	1 mL
1/4 tsp	black pepper	1 mL
Pinch	ground nutmeg	Pinch

PASTRY

10	sheets phyllo pastry	10
1/3 cup	melted butter or olive oil (or more)	75 mL
1/3 cup	dry bread crumbs	75 mL

1. To prepare filling, heat oil in a large skillet over medium heat. Add onions and cook, stirring occasionally, for 4 minutes. Remove from heat and let cool for 20 minutes.

2. In a large bowl, combine onions, green onions, parsley, dill, mint, chicken, spinach, cheese, eggs, salt, pepper and nutmeg. Mix thoroughly.

3. To assemble pie, cut phyllo sheets in half lengthwise. In an 11-inch (28 cm) tart pan with removable bottom or a deep 10-inch (25 cm) pie plate, arrange 10 half sheets (keep remaining phyllo covered with a lightly dampened tea towel) in a spoke-like fashion, brushing each sheet lightly with melted butter and sprinkling with bread crumbs. Ends of phyllo sheets will hang over edges. (Try to work quickly, as phyllo will dry out.)

4. Spoon filling into pastry-lined pan. Layer remaining 10 half phyllo sheets over filling in same spoke-like fashion, brushing with butter and sprinkling with bread crumbs after each layer. Fold in overlapping ends to create "crust." Brush top with remaining butter. With a sharp knife, cut through top layers to mark serving portions.

5. If using a pan with a removable bottom, place pie on a baking sheet. Convection bake or roast in a preheated 350°F (180°C) oven for 35 to 40 minutes, or until golden brown. Let stand for 5 minutes before serving.

Olives with Fennel and Orange
Heat $\frac{1}{4}$ cup (50 mL) olive oil in a large skillet over medium heat. Add 3 thinly sliced cloves garlic, 1 fennel bulb (cut in 1-inch/2.5 cm pieces), pinch hot pepper flakes and 8 strips orange zest. Cook, stirring, for 4 minutes, or until fennel softens. Stir in 2 cups (500 mL) assorted olives, 2 roasted red peppers (cut in 1-inch/2.5 cm pieces) and 2 tbsp (25 mL) chopped sun-dried tomatoes. Stir and cook for 4 minutes. Spoon into a serving dish and sprinkle with 2 tbsp (25 mL) shredded fresh basil. Serve at room temperature or cover and refrigerate for up to two days. Bring to room temperature before serving. Makes 8 servings.

Chickpea and Vegetable Curry

MAKES 4
TO 5 SERVINGS

These days many people are opting for vegetarian eating styles, so it's good to have a few meatless main dishes in your repertoire.

Don't let the word curry scare you. This dish is flavorful without being overspiced. Choose a curry powder that suits your taste — they range from mild to hot.

2 tbsp	olive oil	25 mL
2	onions, chopped	2
1	stalk celery, chopped	1
3	cloves garlic, finely chopped	3
1 tbsp	chopped gingerroot	15 mL
1 tbsp	curry powder	15 mL
¾ tsp	salt	4 mL
2 cups	tomato juice	500 mL
1 cup	cauliflower florets	250 mL
1 cup	diced green beans	250 mL
1	19-oz (540 mL) can chickpeas, drained and rinsed	1
2 tbsp	chopped fresh cilantro or parsley	25 mL

Make Ahead
Curry can be made up to a day ahead, covered and refrigerated. Bring to room temperature before reheating. Convection bake in a preheated 350°F (180°C) oven for 25 minutes.

1. In a large skillet, heat oil over medium heat. Add onions, celery, garlic and ginger. Cook, stirring occasionally, for 8 minutes. Stir in curry powder and salt. Cook for 30 seconds.

2. Stir in tomato juice, cauliflower, beans and chickpeas. Bring to a boil. Transfer to a lightly greased 8-inch (2 L) square baking dish.

3. Convection bake in a preheated 350°F (180°C) oven for 35 to 40 minutes, or until vegetables are just tender. Stir occasionally. Sprinkle with cilantro before serving.

Roasted Cauliflower
Roast leftover cauliflower to make an easy vegetable dish. Cut cauliflower into florets and toss with olive oil, salt and pepper. Place on a parchment-lined baking sheet and convection roast in a preheated 375°F (190°C) oven for 25 to 30 minutes, or until tender. Stir once during cooking.

Vegetables and Salads

Broccoli Cheddar Gratin *96*

Colcannon Bake *97*

Summer Peppers *98*

Roasted Rosemary Potatoes *99*

Turnip and Apple Mash *100*

Stuffed Baked Tomatoes *101*

Roasted Mixed Vegetables *102*

Mediterranean Vegetables with Orzo *103*

Zucchini with Mushroom Stuffing *104*

Potato and Bean Caesar Salad *105*

Warm Chèvre Salad with Mexican Pesto *106*

Roasted Portobello Mushroom and Fennel Salad *108*

Roasted Pear Salad with Candied Pecans
and Blue Cheese *110*

Greek Salad in Kaiser Crouton Cups *112*

Broccoli Cheddar Gratin

MAKES 5
TO 6 SERVINGS

Simply steamed and drizzled with olive oil and lemon juice, broccoli adds both color and texture to the dinner plate; however, this gratin is a great accompaniment for a roast chicken or sliced cold meats. (In France, a vegetable gratin is often served as a main dish with a simple green salad and crusty bread.)

Cauliflower, Brussels sprouts and cabbage can be used instead of broccoli.

Make Ahead

Cool cheese sauce for about a half hour (to prevent broccoli from becoming soggy). Pour sauce over broccoli. Add topping. Cover loosely and refrigerate for up to four hours. Bake for 20 to 25 minutes.

1	large bunch broccoli (about 1 ½ lbs/750 g), cut in 2-inch (5 cm) pieces	1
2 tbsp	butter	25 mL
1	onion, chopped	1
3 tbsp	all-purpose flour	45 mL
2 cups	milk	500 mL
½ tsp	salt	2 mL
¼ tsp	black pepper	1 mL
Pinch	ground nutmeg	Pinch
1 cup	grated Cheddar cheese	250 mL
⅓ cup	fresh bread crumbs	75 mL
⅓ cup	grated Parmesan cheese	75 mL

1. In a medium saucepan, bring ½ inch (1 cm) water to a boil. Add broccoli and steam, covered, for 3 to 4 minutes, or until just tender. Drain. Rinse with cold water. Drain very well. Place in a lightly greased 8-inch (2 L) square baking dish.

2. Meanwhile, to prepare sauce, melt butter in a medium saucepan over medium heat. Add onion and cook for 2 minutes. Add flour and cook, stirring, for 2 minutes, but do not let color.

3. Remove pan from heat and whisk in milk. Return to medium-high heat and bring just to a boil. Add salt, pepper and nutmeg. Reduce heat to low and simmer for 5 minutes, stirring occasionally.

4. Remove sauce from heat and stir in Cheddar. Pour sauce over broccoli.

5. In a small bowl, combine bread crumbs and Parmesan. Sprinkle over broccoli and sauce. Convection bake in a preheated 375°F (190°C) oven for 15 to 20 minutes, or until top is golden and sauce bubbles at edges.

Colcannon Bake

MAKES 8 SERVINGS

This is an adaptation of Ireland's potato and cabbage dish, traditionally associated with Halloween, but it is good at any time of the year. Serve it with corned beef, baked ham (page 71) or cold sliced meats and a green salad.

2 lbs	potatoes (Yukon gold or all-purpose), peeled and cut in large pieces	1 kg
½ cup	milk	125 mL
1 tsp	salt, divided	5 mL
½ tsp	black pepper, divided	2 mL
2 tbsp	olive oil or butter	25 mL
3	onions, chopped	3
4 cups	chopped cabbage	1 L
1 tsp	caraway seeds (optional)	5 mL
½ tsp	paprika	2 mL

1. In a large saucepan, cover potatoes with plenty of salted water. Bring to a boil and cook for 20 to 25 minutes, or until tender. Drain well. Mash, adding milk, ¼ tsp salt and ¼ tsp pepper.

2. Meanwhile, in a large skillet, heat oil over medium-high heat. Add onions and cook, stirring occasionally, for 6 to 8 minutes, or until softened. Stir half of onions into potatoes.

3. Add cabbage to remaining onions in skillet and cook, stirring occasionally, for 10 to 12 minutes, or until cabbage is softened. Add caraway seeds, if using, remaining ¾ tsp (4 mL) salt and ¼ tsp (1 mL) pepper.

4. Spoon half of potato mixture into a lightly greased 9-inch (2.5 L) square baking dish. Spoon cabbage mixture evenly over potatoes. Spread remaining potato mixture over cabbage. Sprinkle top with paprika.

5. Convection bake in a preheated 350°F (180°C) oven for 35 to 40 minutes, or until hot in center.

Summer Peppers

MAKES 6 SERVINGS

The slow roasting in this recipe releases the sweet flavors of the peppers. This dish is perfect for luncheons, buffets and picnics, if carefully packed. Serve hot or at room temperature.

Make Ahead
Bake up to four hours in advance and serve at room temperature.

3	red or yellow bell peppers, halved lengthwise and seeded	3
3	medium tomatoes, cored and cut in wedges	3
1 tbsp	capers	15 mL
3	cloves garlic, thinly sliced	3
1/4 cup	shredded fresh basil	50 mL
1/2 cup	dry bread crumbs	125 mL
1/2 tsp	salt	2 mL
1/4 tsp	black pepper	1 mL
2 tbsp	olive oil	25 mL

1. Arrange peppers cut side up in a single layer in a lightly greased shallow baking dish just large enough to hold peppers in one layer.

2. Place tomatoes, capers and garlic in pepper cavities. Sprinkle with basil, bread crumbs, salt and pepper. Drizzle olive oil over top.

3. Convection bake in a preheated 325°F (160°C) oven for 50 to 60 minutes, or until peppers are softened and partially collapsed.

Roasted Rosemary Potatoes

MAKES 6 SERVINGS

These roasted potatoes will become your new in-house replacement for French fries, without the fuss of deep-frying. The hardest part is to stop eating them. Sometimes I cut them into sticks and serve with garlic mayonnaise as an appetizer.

3 lbs	small new potatoes	1.5 kg
2 tbsp	olive oil	25 mL
1 tsp	salt	5 mL
½ tsp	black pepper	2 mL
2 tbsp	coarsely chopped fresh rosemary, or 1 tsp (5 mL) dried	25 mL
4	cloves garlic, thinly sliced	4

1. Cut potatoes into 1-inch (2.5 cm) pieces (if potatoes are small, leave whole) and place in a large bowl. Toss with olive oil, salt and pepper. Place on two parchment-lined baking sheets in a single layer. Do not crowd potatoes.

2. Convection roast in a preheated 425°F (220°C) oven for 20 minutes. Stir in rosemary and garlic. Continue to roast for 15 to 20 minutes, or until potatoes are golden, crispy and tender. Stir occasionally.

Variation

Roasted Sweet Potatoes: Peel 5 medium sweet potatoes (about 2½ lbs/1.25 kg total) and cut into fingers about 3 inches (7.5 cm) long and ½ inch (1 cm) thick. Place in a large bowl and toss with 2 tbsp (25 mL) olive oil, ¾ tsp (4 mL) salt, ½ tsp (2 mL) black pepper and ½ tsp (2 mL) paprika. Arrange in a single layer on a parchment-lined baking sheet and convection roast in a preheated 425°F (220°C) oven for 25 to 30 minutes, until tender and golden. Stir gently two or three times during roasting. Makes 5 to 6 servings.

Turnip and Apple Mash

MAKES 4
TO 5 SERVINGS

In this recipe, apples lighten the sometimes strong taste of turnip. This dish can easily be doubled or tripled to serve a crowd, especially for Thanksgiving or Christmas get-togethers.

Make Ahead

Assemble dish completely, cover and refrigerate overnight. Bring to room temperature before baking.

1	turnip (about 2½ lbs/1.25 kg), peeled and cut in ½-inch (1 cm) pieces	1
2	apples, peeled, cored and cut in 1-inch (2.5 cm) pieces	2
2 tbsp	packed brown sugar	25 mL
2 tbsp	butter	25 mL
¼ tsp	salt	1 mL
¼ tsp	black pepper	1 mL
¾ cup	fresh bread crumbs	175 mL
½ tsp	paprika	2 mL
2 tbsp	melted butter or olive oil	25 mL

1. Cook turnip in a large saucepan of boiling salted water until almost tender, about 25 to 30 minutes. Add apples and cook until both turnip and apples are tender, about 5 to 7 minutes. Drain very well.

2. Mash turnip and apples with brown sugar, butter, salt and pepper. Spoon into a lightly greased 8-inch (2 L) square baking dish.

3. In a small bowl, combine bread crumbs, paprika and melted butter. Sprinkle bread crumbs over turnip. Convection bake in a preheated 350°F (180°C) oven for 20 to 25 minutes, or until heated through and top is golden.

Stuffed Baked Tomatoes

MAKES 6 SERVINGS

When tomatoes are in season, nothing could be simpler than sliced ripe tomatoes with fresh basil, but for a more substantial dish, try serving these as an appetizer or side dish. Be sure to select firm tomatoes and handle them gently. If you are making this dish during the winter months, buy large vine-ripened tomatoes.

You can replace the couscous with leftover rice in this recipe. Use 1¼ cups (300 mL) cooked rice.

Make Ahead
These tomatoes are also excellent served at room temperature.

6	firm medium to large tomatoes	6
½ cup	uncooked instant couscous	125 mL
2	green onions, chopped	2
2 tbsp	chopped fresh dillweed, tarragon or basil	25 mL
1	clove garlic, minced	1
¼ cup	grated Parmesan cheese	50 mL
½ tsp	salt	2 mL
¼ tsp	black pepper	1 mL
2 tbsp	olive oil	25 mL

1. Cut one quarter off blossom ends of tomatoes. Reserve tops. Carefully remove pulp (a grapefruit spoon works well). Chop pulp.

2. In a bowl, combine chopped tomato pulp, couscous, green onions, dill, garlic, Parmesan, salt and pepper.

3. Arrange tomatoes cut side up in a lightly greased baking dish just large enough to hold tomatoes in one layer. Spoon filling mixture into tomatoes. Place tops over filling. Brush tomatoes with olive oil.

4. Convection bake in a preheated 350°F (180°C) oven for 25 minutes, or until couscous is softened. Cover with foil and let stand for 15 minutes, then carefully remove to a serving platter.

Roasted Mixed Vegetables

MAKES 6 SERVINGS

The convection oven makes roasted vegetables crisp on the outside while enhancing their natural sweetness, and cooking all the vegetables together makes easy work and clean-up for the cook. Puree any leftover vegetables with chicken stock for a quick soup, or toss with a simple balsamic vinaigrette (page 108) for a roasted vegetable salad.

1	medium butternut squash (about 1½ lbs/750 g), peeled and seeded	1
2	medium sweet potatoes (about 1 lb/500 g total), peeled	2
3	parsnips (about 1 lb/500 g total), peeled	3
1	large red onion, peeled	1
10	small new potatoes (about 1¼ lbs/625 g total)	10
2 tbsp	olive oil	25 mL
½ tsp	dried herbs (such as thyme, oregano or marjoram)	2 mL
¾ tsp	salt	4 mL
¼ tsp	black pepper	1 mL

1. Cut squash, sweet potatoes, parsnips and onion into 1½-inch (4 cm) pieces. Combine in a bowl with potatoes, olive oil, herbs, salt and pepper. Toss well. Spread in a single layer on a large parchment-lined baking sheet.

2. Convection roast in a preheated 400°F (200°C) oven for 35 minutes, or until vegetables are just tender. Stir 2 or 3 times during cooking, burying onions under other vegetables if they are browning too quickly.

Oven Thai Rice
In a medium saucepan, heat 2 tbsp (25 mL) vegetable oil over medium heat. Add 1 chopped onion, 2 finely chopped cloves garlic and 1 tbsp (15 mL) finely chopped gingerroot. Cook, stirring, until softened, about 2 minutes. Stir in 1 cup (250 mL) uncooked and rinsed Thai scented or jasmine rice, 2 cups (500 mL) chicken stock and 1 tbsp (15 mL) fish sauce. Bring to a boil. Transfer to a 6-cup (1.5 L) baking dish. Cover.

Bake in a preheated 325°F (160°C) oven for 20 to 25 minutes, or until liquid is just absorbed. Gently stir in 1½ cups (375 mL) diced fresh or canned pineapple, 3 chopped green onions and ¼ cup (50 mL) chopped fresh cilantro. Makes 5 servings.

Mediterranean Vegetables with Orzo

MAKES 8 SERVINGS

Orzo is a rice-shaped pasta often used in soups or pilafs. If it is difficult to find, use 1½ cups (375 mL) cooked long-grain white or brown rice. Serve this as a meatless main course or side dish at a pot-luck or buffet (it can be served hot or at room temperature). The combination is reminiscent of ratatouille, a robust Provençal vegetable stew.

Sicilian (round) or Asian (long slender) eggplants can be used in this dish. Eggplant absorbs oil like a sponge, but try to refrain from adding more. For a juicier dish, add one or two more tomatoes or another zucchini.

Make Ahead
Vegetables can be roasted, covered and refrigerated a day ahead. Reheat at 350°F (180°C) for 20 minutes before combining with hot pasta.

2	onions, cut in 1-inch (2.5 cm) chunks	2
4	cloves garlic, peeled and halved	4
1	eggplant (about 1 lb/250 g), cut in 1-inch (2.5 cm) pieces	1
1	medium zucchini (about 8 oz/250 g), sliced	1
2	red bell peppers, seeded and cut in 1-inch (2.5 cm) pieces	2
3	large tomatoes, cored and cut in 1-inch (2.5 cm) pieces	3
¼ cup	olive oil	50 mL
¾ tsp	herbes de Provence (page 23) or dried thyme	4 mL
½ tsp	salt	2 mL
½ tsp	black pepper	2 mL
½ cup	uncooked orzo	125 mL
1 cup	crumbled chèvre or feta cheese (about 6 oz/175 g)	250 mL
½ cup	pitted black olives	125 mL
¼ cup	shredded fresh basil	50 mL

1. Place onions, garlic, eggplant, zucchini, red peppers and tomatoes in a 13- by 9-inch (3 L) baking dish. Sprinkle with olive oil, herbes de Provence, salt and pepper and toss together.

2. Convection bake in a preheated 400°F (200°C) oven for 45 to 50 minutes, or until vegetables are tender and golden. Stir several times during roasting.

3. Meanwhile, cook orzo in plenty of boiling salted water for about 8 minutes, or until tender. Drain well.

4. Toss vegetables with orzo and sprinkle with chèvre, olives and basil.

Zucchini with Mushroom Stuffing

MAKES 4 SERVINGS

Zucchini make ideal containers for stuffings. Using a food processor speeds up the chopping process, but avoid overprocessing the mushrooms (the grating disc does a good job of "chopping" mushrooms).

Make Ahead
Zucchini can be prepared, covered and refrigerated for up to eight hours. Let stand at room temperature for a half hour before baking.

4	medium zucchini (about 8 oz/250 g each)	4
2 tbsp	butter or olive oil	25 mL
1	onion, chopped	1
8 oz	mushrooms, finely chopped	250 g
3/4 tsp	salt	4 mL
1/4 tsp	black pepper	1 mL
1/4 tsp	dried thyme leaves	1 mL
1/2 cup	fresh bread crumbs	125 mL
1/3 cup	grated Parmesan cheese	75 mL
1/4 cup	chopped fresh parsley	50 mL

1. Halve zucchini lengthwise. Using a sharp measuring spoon or melon baller, scoop out flesh to make a container that will hold stuffing. Chop zucchini flesh by hand or in a food processor.

2. In a large skillet, heat butter over medium-high heat. Add onion and cook for 3 minutes. Add mushrooms and chopped zucchini. Cook, stirring occasionally, for 10 minutes, or until all moisture has evaporated. Add salt, pepper and thyme.

3. Transfer filling to a bowl to cool slightly. Stir in bread crumbs, Parmesan and parsley.

4. Arrange zucchini on a baking sheet. Spoon in filling, mounding in center. Convection bake in a preheated 400°F (200°C) oven for 15 to 20 minutes, or until zucchini is tender and filling is hot.

Pita Croutons
Sprinkle these croutons on soups or salads.

Cut three 7-inch (18 cm) pita breads into 1-inch (2.5 cm) pieces. Place on a baking sheet in a single layer. Convection bake in a preheated 300°F (150°C) oven for 12 to 15 minutes, or until crisp. Stir once during baking. Makes about 4 1/2 cups (1.125 L).

Potato and Bean Caesar Salad

MAKES 6 SERVINGS

Caesar salad, a perennial favorite, shows up in many variations. An excellent year-round salad, this version is especially good during the summer months when baby new potatoes and beans are in season.

Make Ahead

Roast vegetables up to six hours in advance and keep at room temperature. Dressing can be prepared, covered and refrigerated for up to two days.

2 lbs	new potatoes	1 kg
6 tsp	olive oil, divided	30 mL
8 oz	green beans, trimmed and cut in half	250 g
1/2 tsp	salt, divided	2 mL
1/2 tsp	black pepper, divided	2 mL
CAESAR DRESSING		
2	cloves garlic, minced	2
2	anchovy fillets, mashed, or 1 tsp (5 mL) anchovy paste	2
1 tsp	Dijon mustard	5 mL
3 tbsp	lemon juice	45 mL
1/2 tsp	Worcestershire sauce	2 mL
1/4 cup	olive oil	50 mL
2 tbsp	grated Parmesan cheese	25 mL
1/2 tsp	salt	2 mL
1/2 tsp	black pepper	2 mL
SALAD		
1/2	head Romaine lettuce, shredded	1/2
2	tomatoes, cut in sections	2
6	slices cooked bacon, crumbled	6
2 tbsp	grated Parmesan cheese	25 mL

1. Cut potatoes into 1-inch (2.5 cm) pieces and place in a large bowl. Toss with 4 tsp (20 mL) olive oil, 1/4 tsp (1 mL) salt and 1/4 tsp (1 mL) pepper. Place on a parchment-lined baking sheet. Toss beans with remaining 2 tsp (10 mL) olive oil, 1/4 tsp (1 mL) salt and 1/4 tsp (1 mL) pepper. Place on another parchment-lined baking sheet. Convection roast vegetables in a preheated 400°F (200°C) oven. Remove beans from oven after 15 minutes. Cook potatoes for an additional 20 minutes, or until tender. Cool potatoes and beans to room temperature.

2. Meanwhile, to prepare dressing, in a small bowl, whisk together garlic, anchovies, mustard, lemon juice, Worcestershire, olive oil, Parmesan, salt and pepper.

3. Toss lettuce with half the dressing. Toss potatoes and beans with remaining dressing. Spoon vegetables and tomatoes over lettuce. Sprinkle with bacon and Parmesan.

Warm Chèvre Salad with Mexican Pesto

MAKES 6 SERVINGS

Although this salad consists of several steps, most can be prepared in advance. The Mexican pesto yields more than is required for the salad, so use the extra to toss with steamed vegetables, pasta or whisk into a vinaigrette.

Pumpkin seeds are available in health food and bulk food stores.

Make Ahead
Pesto can be prepared a day ahead. Cover and refrigerate. Tomatoes can be roasted up to four hours in advance and kept at room temperature. Roll cheese in tortilla chips and refrigerate until baking.

MEXICAN PESTO

½ cup	pumpkin seeds, toasted	125 mL
½ cup	lightly packed fresh cilantro leaves	125 mL
2	green onions, coarsely chopped	2
2	cloves garlic, chopped	2
2 tsp	chopped jalapeño pepper (or to taste)	10 mL
½ tsp	salt	2 mL
3 tbsp	olive oil	45 mL
2 tbsp	water	25 mL

WARM CHÈVRE SALAD

3	medium tomatoes, cored and halved crosswise	3
1 tbsp	olive oil	15 mL
¼ tsp	salt	1 mL
¼ tsp	black pepper	1 mL
10 oz	chèvre, cut in 6 pieces	300 g
½ cup	crushed tortilla chips	125 mL
6 cups	arugula or shredded Romaine lettuce	1.5 L

1. To prepare pesto, place pumpkin seeds, cilantro, green onions, garlic, jalapeños and salt in a food processor or blender and process until coarsely chopped. Add olive oil and water. Process until pureed.

2. To prepare salad, arrange tomatoes in a shallow baking dish large enough to hold tomatoes in a single layer (cut small pieces from bottoms so tomatoes sit upright).

3. Sprinkle tomatoes with oil, salt and pepper. Convection bake in a preheated 400°F (200°C) oven for 10 to 12 minutes, or until tomatoes are softened but still hold their shape.

4. Roll chèvre in crushed tortilla chips, flattening each piece slightly. Place on a parchment-lined baking sheet. Convection bake in a preheated 400°F (200°C) oven for 6 minutes. (Tomatoes and chèvre can be cooked at same time.)

5. To serve, arrange arugula on serving plates. Place tomato on greens. Arrange chèvre on top of tomato. Place a generous serving of pesto on top of chèvre.

Toasting Nuts and Seeds

Place nuts or seeds in a small baking dish. Convection bake in a preheated 300°F (150°C) oven for 5 to 10 minutes, or until golden. Toasting time depends on nut and seed size (bake pumpkin seeds for 5 to 6 minutes, or until seeds pop).

Roasted Portobello Mushroom and Fennel Salad

MAKES 6 SERVINGS

Portobello mushrooms appear in soups, salads, side dishes and main courses. Although not a complete protein, they are often the mainstay of vegetarian menus, perhaps because of their meaty texture. If you wish, you can use a spoon to scrape away the dark gills on the underside of the mushrooms.

Make Ahead
Prepare dressing, cover and refrigerate for up to two days.

MUSHROOMS AND FENNEL

1/3 cup	olive oil	75 mL
4	cloves garlic, minced	4
2 tsp	chopped fresh tarragon, or 3/4 tsp (4 mL) dried	10 mL
1/2 tsp	salt	2 mL
1/4 tsp	black pepper	1 mL
6	portobello mushrooms (about 1 1/2 lbs/750 g total), stems removed	6
1	large bulb fennel (about 1 1/2 lbs/750 g), trimmed and cut in 12 wedges	1

BALSAMIC VINAIGRETTE

2 tbsp	balsamic vinegar	25 mL
1 tbsp	lemon juice	15 mL
1 tsp	Dijon mustard	5 mL
2 tbsp	olive oil	25 mL
1/4 tsp	salt	1 mL
1/4 tsp	black pepper	1 mL

SALAD

6 cups	arugula or baby spinach	1.5 L
1/2 cup	toasted pine nuts (page 107)	125 mL

1. In a small bowl, whisk together olive oil, garlic, tarragon, salt and pepper.

2. Arrange mushrooms, round side up, on a parchment-lined baking sheet. Brush with half the oil mixture.

3. In a large bowl, toss fennel wedges with remaining oil mixture. Place on another parchment-lined baking sheet.

4. Convection roast mushrooms and fennel in a preheated 400°F (200°C) oven — mushrooms for 12 minutes, fennel for 18 to 20 minutes, or until tender. Cool both slightly. Cut each mushroom diagonally into 4 slices.

5. To prepare vinaigrette, in a small bowl or measuring cup, whisk together vinegar, lemon juice, mustard, olive oil, salt and pepper.
6. Toss arugula with vinaigrette and arrange on serving plates. Arrange mushrooms and fennel over greens. Sprinkle with pine nuts.

Fontina and Grape Flatbread

Serve this as an appetizer or with soups or salads.

Defrost half a 14-oz (397 g) package frozen puff pastry. On a lightly floured surface, roll pastry into a 16- by 6-inch (40 by 15 cm) rectangle. Place on a parchment-lined baking sheet and crimp edges slightly.

Spread pastry with $1\frac{1}{2}$ cups (375 mL) diced or grated Fontina cheese. Top with $1\frac{1}{4}$ cups (300 mL) halved red seedless grapes and 2 tsp (10 mL) chopped fresh rosemary.

Convection bake in a preheated 375°F (190°C) oven for 15 to 18 minutes, or until pastry is cooked and golden brown (underside of pastry should be golden).

Gently slide pastry onto a rack and cool for 5 minutes. Cut into serving pieces. Makes 10 to 12 slices.

Roasted Pear Salad with Candied Pecans and Blue Cheese

MAKES 6 SERVINGS

This is the salad to serve at a special dinner party. We prepared a version of this for a fundraising dinner for 350 guests, and could have raised even more had we sold the recipe! The pears should be ripe but firm. The roasted pears can also be served on their own with baked ham, chicken or pork.

Make Ahead
Pears and pecans can be cooked up to six hours ahead. Store pecans in a dry place (away from humidity and nibblers!).

PEARS

3	pears (Bartlett or Anjou), halved, peeled and cored	3
2 tbsp	olive oil	25 mL
¼ tsp	dried thyme or oregano leaves	1 mL
¼ tsp	salt	1 mL
¼ tsp	black pepper	1 mL

CANDIED PECANS

1 cup	pecan halves	250 mL
2 tbsp	granulated sugar	25 mL
2 tbsp	liquid honey	25 mL
2 tbsp	boiling water	25 mL
½ tsp	dried rosemary leaves	2 mL
¼ tsp	salt	1 mL

RASPBERRY VINAIGRETTE

2 tbsp	olive oil	25 mL
2 tbsp	raspberry vinegar	25 mL
1 tsp	Dijon mustard	5 mL
¼ tsp	salt	1 mL
¼ tsp	black pepper	1 mL

SALAD

8 cups	baby salad greens	2 L
½ cup	crumbled blue cheese (about 3 oz/90 g)	125 mL
1 cup	fresh raspberries	250 mL

1. Place pears cut side up in a shallow baking dish. Sprinkle with olive oil, thyme, salt and pepper. Turn to coat with oil.

2. Convection roast in a preheated 325°F (160°C) oven for 20 to 25 minutes, or until pears are just tender. Cool to room temperature.

3. Meanwhile, in a bowl, combine pecan halves with sugar, honey, boiling water, rosemary and salt. Stir well and spoon onto a parchment-lined baking sheet.

4. Convection roast nuts in a preheated 325°F (160°C) oven for 16 to 18 minutes, or until nuts are golden and water has evaporated. Stir twice during cooking. Cool until easy to handle. Loosen from paper.

5. To prepare vinaigrette, whisk together olive oil, vinegar, mustard, salt and pepper.

6. Toss greens with dressing and arrange on individual serving plates. Place pear in center of greens. Fill cavity with cheese. Sprinkle with pecans and raspberries.

Pears
When in season, pears ripen quickly, but during the winter months they often take time to ripen at room temperature. To help this process, place unripe pears in a brown paper bag with one or two apples, sealing tightly and checking daily. Once they are ripe, use immediately or store in the refrigerator.

Greek Salad in Kaiser Crouton Cups

MAKES 6 SERVINGS

I also serve thick soups, beans and stews in these edible cups. Let the salad overflow onto the serving plate (the salad can also be served on its own).

Make Ahead

Crouton cups can be prepared up to six hours ahead. Cover loosely to prevent them from drying out too much.

CROUTON CUPS

6	large Kaiser rolls	6
¼ cup	olive oil	50 mL
2	cloves garlic, minced	2

GREEK SALAD

2 cups	chopped iceberg lettuce	500 mL
1 cup	diced cucumber	250 mL
2	tomatoes, cored, seeded and cut in ½-inch (1 cm) pieces	2
1	small red bell pepper, seeded and cut in ½-inch (1 cm) pieces	1
½ cup	chopped red onion	125 mL
2 tbsp	chopped fresh mint	25 mL
¾ cup	feta cheese, crumbled (about 4 oz/125 g)	175 mL
½ cup	black olives	125 mL

DRESSING

3 tbsp	olive oil	45 mL
2 tbsp	lemon juice	25 mL
1 tbsp	chopped fresh oregano, or ½ tsp (2 mL) dried	15 mL
¼ tsp	salt	1 mL
¼ tsp	black pepper	1 mL

1. For the crouton cups, cut top third from each roll. Pull out center from each roll (use to make bread crumbs) to make a hollow.

2. Combine olive oil and garlic and brush bottom of tops and inside of cups. Place rolls on a baking sheet and convection bake in a preheated 325°F (160°C) oven for 6 to 8 minutes, or until crusty. Remove from oven and let cool to room temperature.

3. For the salad, in a large bowl, combine lettuce, cucumber, tomatoes, red pepper, onion, mint, feta and olives.

4. To make dressing, whisk together olive oil, lemon juice, oregano, salt and pepper. Toss salad with dressing. Spoon salad into and around cups. Serve lids on the side.

Breakfast, Brunch and Lunch

Rise and Shine Granola *114*

Oven French Toast with Caramelized Apples *115*

Brie and Strawberry Crêpes *116*

Asparagus, Chèvre and Smoked Salmon Frittata *118*

Prosciutto Onion Quiche *119*

Oven Home Fries with Peameal Bacon *120*

Mushroom and Bacon Open-face Sandwich *121*

Easy Cheese Soufflé *122*

Tofu with Sesame Hoisin Glaze *123*

Homemade Pizza *124*

Vegetable Strudel *126*

Rise and Shine Granola

MAKES 8 CUPS (2 L)

With so many cereal products on the market, is a homemade granola really necessary? I think so, as you can control exactly what goes into it and make substitutions according to your own taste and nutritional needs. This granola is so good, many people eat it as a snack.

For gifts, package it in plastic bags with colorful ribbons and homemade labels (a great project for young cooks).

Make Ahead

The granola can be made and stored in an airtight container for up to two weeks.

3 cups	rolled oats (not instant), divided	750 mL
1 cup	whole almonds, with skins	250 mL
1 cup	pecan halves or hazelnuts	250 mL
1 cup	unsweetened shredded coconut	250 mL
1 cup	wheat germ	250 mL
½ cup	sesame seeds	125 mL
½ cup	pumpkin seeds	125 mL
½ cup	unsalted sunflower seeds	125 mL
⅓ cup	vegetable oil	75 mL
⅓ cup	liquid honey	75 mL

1. Place 1½ cups (375 mL) rolled oats, almonds and pecans in a food processor. Pulse several times until coarsely chopped.

2. In a large bowl, combine chopped oat mixture with remaining 1½ cups (375 mL) rolled oats, coconut, wheat germ, sesame seeds, pumpkin seeds and sunflower seeds. Add oil and honey and combine thoroughly.

3. Spread granola over two parchment-lined baking sheets. Convection bake in a preheated 300°F (150°C) oven for 15 minutes, or until golden. Stir occasionally. Cool completely.

Oven French Toast with Caramelized Apples

MAKES 4 SERVINGS

The beauty of making French toast in the oven is the ease of cooking in one operation, rather than continuous pan-frying. Select an apple that holds its shape well, such as Northern Spy, Ida Red or Golden Delicious. Thickly sliced egg bread or cinnamon bread gives the best results; my second choice would be potato bread (page 137). Other toppings could be seasonal fresh fruit such as sliced strawberries, blueberries, sliced peaches and even diced pineapple in winter months.

Make Ahead
Apples can be prepared, covered and refrigerated up to a day ahead. Reheat at 375°F (190°C) for 12 minutes, or until hot.

CARAMELIZED APPLES

5	apples, peeled, cored and sliced	5
1/3 cup	packed brown sugar	75 mL
2 tbsp	butter, melted	25 mL
1 tsp	grated orange zest	5 mL
1/4 tsp	ground cinnamon	1 mL

FRENCH TOAST

3	eggs	3
3/4 cup	milk	175 mL
2 tbsp	granulated sugar	25 mL
1/2 tsp	vanilla	2 mL
6	slices bread (about 3/4 inch/2 cm thick)	6

1. To prepare apples, in a large bowl, combine apples, brown sugar, melted butter, orange zest and cinnamon. Spoon into a lightly greased 8-inch (2 L) square baking dish.

2. To prepare French toast, in a large shallow dish, beat together eggs, milk, granulated sugar and vanilla. Add bread slices, turning gently to absorb liquid. Arrange on a lightly buttered parchment-lined baking sheet.

3. Convection bake apples and bread in a preheated 375°F (190°C) oven for 25 minutes, or until toast is golden and slightly crispy. Turn toast once during cooking. Stir apples gently twice during cooking (do not mash apples).

4. To serve, cut toast in half diagonally. Spoon apples on toast.

Brie and Strawberry Crêpes

MAKES 10
TO 12 CRÊPES

It may take a couple of sample crêpes to arrive at the right heat for the pan and the correct swirl of the batter. I often sprinkle the samples with a little lemon juice and granulated sugar, roll up like a cigar and eat as a cook's bonus.

If you are in a hurry, prepared crêpes are available in some supermarkets and specialty food shops.

Make Ahead

Crêpes can be made ahead, wrapped tightly and frozen for up to six weeks. Complete dish can be assembled up to eight hours ahead, covered and refrigerated. Bring to room temperature before baking.

CRÊPES

3	eggs	3
¾ cup	all-purpose flour	175 mL
¾ cup	milk	175 mL
3 tbsp	butter, melted, divided	45 mL
¼ tsp	salt	1 mL

FILLING

1½ cups	sliced fresh strawberries	375 mL
8 oz	Brie, cut into 12 pieces	250 g
2 tbsp	butter, melted	25 mL

GARNISH

¾ cup	sour cream	175 mL
2 tbsp	granulated sugar	25 mL
1 tsp	grated orange zest	5 mL
1 cup	sliced fresh strawberries	250 mL

1. To prepare crêpes, combine eggs, flour, milk, 2 tbsp (25 mL) melted butter and salt in a food processor or blender. Blend until smooth. Pour into a bowl or large measuring cup.

2. Heat an 8-inch (20 cm) nonstick skillet over medium heat. Brush lightly with some remaining melted butter. Pour a generous 2 tbsp (25 mL) batter into center of pan. Swirl and rotate pan to form crêpe. Cook for 40 seconds, or until top is no longer shiny. Turn and cook second side for 20 seconds. Slide onto plate. Repeat with remaining melted butter and batter to make 10 to 12 crêpes.

3. Arrange crêpes on a flat surface. Spoon about 2 tbsp (25 mL) sliced strawberries in center of each crêpe. Place piece of Brie on top.

4. Fold bottom of crêpe over strawberries and fold in sides. Fold down top of crêpe (like an envelope).

5. Arrange crêpe seam side down in a lightly buttered 13- by 9-inch (3 L) baking dish. Repeat with remaining crêpes, arranging in baking dish in a single layer. Brush with 2 tbsp (25 mL) melted butter.

6. Convection bake in a preheated 300°F (150°C) oven for 12 to 14 minutes, or until just heated through. Top will be slightly crispy.

7. For garnish, in a small bowl, combine sour cream, sugar and orange zest. Serve on side with sliced strawberries.

Variations

Ricotta Orange Crêpes: In a large bowl, combine 3 cups (750 mL) ricotta cheese, 1 beaten egg, 3 tbsp (45 mL) packed brown sugar, 1 tbsp (15 mL) all-purpose flour, 1 tbsp (15 mL) orange juice concentrate and 1 tsp (5 mL) grated orange zest. Mix thoroughly. Fill each crêpe with a scant ¼ cup (50 mL) filling. Serve crêpes with 2 cups (500 mL) sliced strawberries.

Mushroom, Spinach and Ham Crêpes: Melt 2 tbsp (25 mL) butter in a large skillet over medium-high heat. Add 1 chopped onion and 2 cups (500 mL) sliced mushrooms and cook for 6 minutes, or until liquid evaporates. Spoon into a large bowl and cool. Add 1 cup (250 mL) diced ham, 1 cup (250 mL) grated Gruyère cheese, 1 10-oz (300 g) package frozen chopped spinach (defrosted and squeezed dry), 2 tbsp (25 mL) chopped fresh dillweed, ¼ tsp (1 mL) salt and ¼ tsp (1 mL) black pepper. Combine thoroughly. Fill each crêpe with a scant ¼ cup (50 mL) filling. Sprinkle filled crêpes with ¼ cup (50 mL) grated Parmesan cheese before baking.

Asparagus, Chèvre and Smoked Salmon Frittata

MAKES 4
TO 6 SERVINGS

The traditional frittata is usually started on the stove and finished in the oven, but in this recipe the frittata is baked like a crustless quiche. Most of the preparation can be done ahead; just whip up a quick salad while the frittata cooks.

This is an excellent springtime dish. For a vegetarian version, omit the salmon.

Cut leftovers into cubes or slice to serve on top of a salad or in a sandwich.

Make Ahead
Prepare all ingredients up to six hours in advance, cover and refrigerate. Assemble just before baking.

1 lb	fresh asparagus	500 g
2 tbsp	butter	25 mL
1	onion, chopped	1
6	eggs	6
¾ cup	crumbled chèvre (about 4 oz/125 g)	175 mL
¾ cup	diced smoked salmon (about 4 oz/125 g)	175 mL
⅓ cup	water	75 mL
2 tbsp	chopped fresh dillweed	25 mL
½ tsp	salt	2 mL
¼ tsp	black pepper	1 mL

1. Break off tough stem ends of asparagus. Cut asparagus into ½-inch (1 cm) pieces. Cook in boiling salted water for 3 minutes, or until tender. Drain and cool under cold running water. Drain well and pat dry with paper towels.

2. In a small skillet, melt butter over medium heat. Add onion. Cook, stirring occasionally, for 4 minutes.

3. In a bowl, beat eggs until blended. Stir in asparagus, onion, chèvre, smoked salmon, water, dill, salt and pepper. Pour mixture into a lightly greased 8-inch (2 L) square baking dish.

4. Convection bake in a preheated 350°F (180°C) oven for 25 to 30 minutes, or until frittata is set in center and top is golden. Let stand for 10 minutes before serving.

Variation
Spinach, Cheddar and Ham Frittata: Instead of asparagus, cook 10 oz (300 g) fresh spinach. Drain, squeeze dry and chop. Instead of chèvre, use 1 cup (250 mL) grated Cheddar or Gruyère cheese. Use diced ham, smoked chicken or turkey instead of the smoked salmon.

Prosciutto Onion Quiche

MAKES 6 SERVINGS

Although quiche comes and goes in fashion, it remains a favorite of many people. Try using different cheeses, cooked vegetables and meats such as ham or smoked salmon. For a vegetarian version, just omit the prosciutto.

Partially prebaking the pastry helps to prevent a soggy bottom crust. The prebaking step can be done up to six hours ahead. Keep the pastry shell at room temperature.

1	unbaked 9-inch (23 cm) pie shell, storebought or homemade (page 160)	1
2 tsp	Dijon mustard	10 mL
1 cup	grated Gruyère cheese	250 mL
2 tbsp	butter	25 mL
2	onions, chopped	2
4	eggs	4
1 ½ cups	sour cream or milk	375 mL
½ tsp	salt	2 mL
¼ tsp	black pepper	1 mL
Pinch	ground nutmeg	Pinch
½ cup	diced prosciutto	125 mL
2 tbsp	chopped fresh basil or parsley	25 mL

1. Line pastry shell with foil or parchment paper and fill with pie weights or dry beans. Convection bake or roast in a preheated 400°F (200°C) oven for 15 to 18 minutes, or until golden around edges. Carefully remove weights and foil. Cool. Brush bottom of crust with mustard and sprinkle with cheese.

2. Meanwhile, in a large skillet, melt butter over medium heat. Add onions and cook until softened and just starting to color, about 5 minutes. Cool slightly.

3. In a large bowl, beat eggs until blended. Stir in sour cream, salt, pepper, nutmeg and onions. Pour into prepared pie shell.

4. Arrange prosciutto and basil over top of quiche. Convection bake or roast in a preheated 350°F (180°C) oven for 25 minutes, or until center is set and top is golden. Let sit for 10 minutes before serving.

Oven Home Fries
with Peameal Bacon

MAKES 5
TO 6 SERVINGS

This dish always reminds me of the hearty specials served at diners. You can add your own touches such as mushrooms, herbs or sun-dried tomatoes. My grandmother cooked home fries in a well-seasoned cast-iron frying pan using bacon fat, stale bread cubes, green onions, sage and leftover cooked potatoes. What a memory.

With the convection oven, trays of home fries can be prepared for a hungry group, with the peameal bacon added to the oven during the last half of the cooking time. Cook extra potatoes the day before to use in this dish (I usually leave the skins on).

2 lbs	cooked potatoes, cut in ½-inch (1 cm) pieces (about 6 cups/1.5 L)	1 kg
3	onions, cut in ½-inch (1 cm) pieces	3
3	cloves garlic, coarsely chopped	3
3 tbsp	olive oil	45 mL
¾ tsp	salt	4 mL
½ tsp	dried marjoram or oregano leaves	2 mL
¼ tsp	black pepper	1 mL
¼ tsp	paprika	1 mL
1½ lbs	peameal bacon, sliced	750 g

1. In a large bowl, toss together potatoes, onions, garlic, olive oil, salt, marjoram, pepper and paprika. Spread in a single layer on a parchment-lined baking sheet.

2. Convection bake in a preheated 425°F (220°C) oven for 30 to 35 minutes, or until golden and slightly crispy. Stir gently twice during cooking.

3. Meanwhile, arrange bacon slices slightly overlapping on a separate parchment-lined baking sheet. Place on another shelf in oven. Cook for 10 to 12 minutes, or until golden around edges. (Timing will depend on thickness of bacon.)

Mushroom and Bacon Open-face Sandwich

MAKES 4 SERVINGS

When I worked at a hotel in Australia, the most popular sandwich was a clubhouse, so bacon was always cooked ahead. Most restaurants "tray" bacon, cooking it slightly overlapping on trays in the oven, then draining off the fat. You can use the same technique in the home convection oven.

8 oz	mushrooms, thinly sliced	250 g
2 tbsp	olive oil	25 mL
2 tbsp	chopped fresh parsley	25 mL
2	cloves garlic, minced	2
1 tsp	chopped fresh tarragon, or ¼ tsp (1 mL) dried	5 mL
¼ tsp	salt	1 mL
¼ tsp	black pepper	1 mL
8	lean slices bacon	8
4	thick slices multigrain, seed or whole wheat bread	4
4	slices provolone or mozzarella cheese	4

1. In a medium bowl, combine mushrooms with olive oil, parsley, garlic, tarragon, salt and pepper. Arrange in a single layer on a parchment-lined baking sheet.

2. Arrange bacon slices on a foil-lined baking sheet.

3. Convection bake mushrooms in a preheated 375°F (190°C) oven for 10 minutes. Add bacon to oven and continue to bake for 12 to 15 minutes, or until bacon is slightly crispy. Remove bacon and mushrooms from oven. Drain bacon on paper towels.

4. Meanwhile, place bread on a baking sheet. Toast in oven for 5 minutes. Turn bread slices.

5. Spoon mushrooms over bread and top with bacon and cheese. Return to oven until cheese melts, about 3 to 4 minutes. Serve hot.

Easy Cheese Soufflé

MAKES 4 SERVINGS

For some reason, soufflés seem to alarm the novice cook. Yet a soufflé is simply a cheese sauce with beaten egg whites folded in before baking. The only tricky part is the timing — guests should be at the table when the soufflé emerges from the oven.

If you do not have a soufflé dish, use a deep casserole with straight sides. Serve with a green salad or steamed asparagus or broccoli. Cut any leftovers into small pieces and serve on top of a salad.

¼ cup	butter	50 mL
¼ cup	all-purpose flour	50 mL
1 ½ cups	hot milk	375 mL
½ tsp	dry mustard	2 mL
¼ tsp	salt	1 mL
¼ tsp	black pepper	1 mL
Pinch	ground nutmeg	Pinch
6	eggs, separated	6
1 cup	grated Cheddar cheese	250 mL
¼ tsp	cream of tartar	1 mL

1. In a large, heavy saucepan, melt butter over medium-low heat. Add flour and cook, stirring, for 3 minutes without browning.

2. Whisk in hot milk, mustard, salt, pepper and nutmeg. Cook, stirring constantly, for 2 minutes until sauce thickens. Remove from heat.

3. In a medium bowl, beat egg yolks. Stir ½ cup (125 mL) hot sauce into yolks. Add yolks back to sauce and cook for 1 minute. Remove from heat and let sit for 10 minutes. Stir in cheese.

4. In a large, very clean bowl, beat egg whites with cream of tartar until stiff (but not dry) peaks form. Stir one quarter of egg whites into cooled cheese base. Then add cheese mixture to remaining egg whites. Gently fold into whites. Turn into a buttered 8-cup (2 L) soufflé dish. Smooth surface.

5. Convection bake in a preheated 325°F (160°C) oven for 35 to 40 minutes, or until top is firm yet soufflé is slightly jiggly. Serve immediately.

Tofu with Sesame Hoisin Glaze

MAKES 4 SERVINGS

Tofu is high in protein and virtually cholesterol free. To encourage family and guests to enjoy tofu, marinate it in flavored sauces rather than serving it plain.

Make Ahead
The tofu and sauce can be prepared and assembled a day ahead. Cover and refrigerate. Let stand at room temperature for a half hour before baking.

1	12-oz (350 g) package extra-firm tofu, patted dry and cut in ½-inch (1 cm) slices	1
3 tbsp	hoisin sauce	45 mL
3 tbsp	orange juice	45 mL
1 tbsp	tomato paste	15 mL
1 tbsp	sesame oil	15 mL
2 tsp	rice vinegar	10 mL
1 tsp	liquid honey or granulated sugar	5 mL
¼ tsp	hot chili paste or hot pepper sauce (optional)	1 mL
1 tbsp	sesame seeds	15 mL
2	green onions, sliced on the diagonal	2

1. Arrange tofu slices in a single layer in a lightly greased 8-inch (2 L) square baking dish.

2. In a bowl, combine hoisin sauce, orange juice, tomato paste, sesame oil, vinegar, honey, chili paste and sesame seeds. Spoon over tofu and turn slices to coat.

3. Convection bake in a preheated 325°F (160°C) oven for 20 to 25 minutes, or until sauce is bubbling. Garnish with green onions.

Variation
Chicken with Sesame Hoisin Glaze: Place four 6-oz (175 g) boneless, skinless chicken breasts in a single layer in baking dish. Prepare sauce and pour over chicken, turning chicken to coat with sauce. Cover and marinate, refrigerated, for up to 4 hours. Arrange chicken on a parchment-lined baking sheet. Spoon sauce over chicken. Convection bake for 25 to 30 minutes, or until juices run clear.

Homemade Pizza

Homemade pizza is easy to make. Use the suggested toppings or substitute your own favorite.

Each topping provides enough for two pizzas (one whole recipe of dough). You can halve the topping recipes to prepare two different pizzas.

For a nice finish, brush the edges of the crust with olive oil as soon as the pizzas come out of the oven.

1	recipe Rosemary Garlic Fougasse (page 138)	1

TOMATO AND MUSHROOM TOPPING

2 tbsp	olive oil	25 mL
4 cups	sliced mushrooms	1 L
¼ tsp	salt	1 mL
¼ tsp	black pepper	1 mL
1 cup	tomato sauce, storebought or homemade (page 80)	250 mL
3 cups	grated mozzarella cheese	750 mL
⅓ cup	grated Parmesan cheese	75 mL

PESTO AND CHÈVRE TOPPING

1½ cups	lightly packed basil leaves	375 mL
1	clove garlic, peeled	1
⅓ cup	grated Parmesan cheese	75 mL
1 tsp	lemon juice	5 mL
2 tbsp	pine nuts (optional)	25 mL
4	tomatoes, thinly sliced	4
¾ cup	crumbled chèvre (about 4 oz/125 g)	175 mL

1. For dough, prepare one recipe Rosemary Garlic Fougasse (omit rosemary and garlic if desired). After dough has risen, divide into two equal portions.

2. On a lightly floured surface, roll each half into a 12-inch (30 cm) circle. (Rest dough occasionally if it springs back.) Place dough on a pizza pan or baking sheet dusted with cornmeal or semolina. Stretch dough gently if it shrinks.

3. To prepare tomato-mushroom topping, heat oil in a large skillet over medium-high heat. Add mushrooms and cook, stirring occasionally, for 10 minutes, or until mushrooms are golden and moisture has evaporated. Season with salt and pepper. Remove from heat and let sit for 10 minutes.

4. To assemble, spread tomato sauce over dough to within 1 inch (2.5 cm) of edge. Sprinkle sauce with mozzarella. Arrange mushrooms over cheese and top with Parmesan.

5. To prepare pesto topping, in a food processor or blender, combine basil, garlic, Parmesan, lemon juice and pine nuts, if using. Process until pureed.

6. To assemble pizza, spread pesto over dough to within 1 inch (2.5 cm) of edge. Arrange tomato slices in a single layer over pesto. Top with chèvre.

7. Convection bake pizzas in a preheated 425°F (220°C) oven for 15 to 18 minutes, or until crust is golden and puffed.

Pizza Topping Ideas

Mix and match your family's favorite toppings, adjusting ingredients to suit specific tastes. Try the following combinations:

- cooked Italian sausage, provolone and roasted peppers
- Fontina, cherry tomatoes and roasted onions
- mozzarella, roasted eggplant and pesto
- tomato sauce, mozzarella and chopped arugula
- chèvre, black olive tapenade and shredded basil

Vegetable Strudel

**MAKES 6
TO 8 SERVINGS**

Perfect for a brunch or luncheon, this strudel can also be served as a dinner side dish or vegetarian main course. If the leeks are large, one would be adequate.

Make Ahead
The filling can be prepared, covered and refrigerated up to a day in advance. The strudel can be rolled, covered and refrigerated up to six hours before baking.

2 tbsp	olive oil	25 mL
2	leeks, white part only, thinly sliced	2
2	cloves garlic, finely chopped	2
1	red bell pepper, seeded and diced	1
1	10-oz (300 g) package frozen chopped spinach, defrosted and squeezed dry	1
1 cup	grated Gruyère or Fontina cheese	250 mL
¼ cup	chopped fresh parsley	50 mL
¼ cup	chopped fresh dillweed	50 mL
½ tsp	salt	2 mL
¼ tsp	black pepper	1 mL
Pinch	ground nutmeg	Pinch
6	sheets phyllo pastry	6
¼ cup	butter, melted	50 mL
¼ cup	dry bread crumbs	50 mL

1. In a large skillet, heat oil over medium-high heat. Add leeks, garlic and pepper and cook, stirring frequently, for 4 minutes, or until softened. Remove vegetables to a large bowl and let stand for 20 minutes.

2. Add spinach, cheese, parsley, dill, salt, pepper and nutmeg to leek mixture. Mix thoroughly.

3. To assemble, place a sheet of phyllo on a flat surface. Brush with some melted butter and sprinkle with some bread crumbs. Place second sheet of phyllo on top of first one. Brush with butter and sprinkle with crumbs. Repeat until all phyllo is used.

4. Spoon filling lengthwise along phyllo about 2 inches (5 cm) from long edge. Roll up pastry to make a long roll. Carefully lift onto a parchment-lined baking sheet, seam side down. Brush with melted butter. Cut 6 to 8 slits in top of strudel to mark serving pieces.

5. Convection bake or roast in a preheated 350°F (180°C) oven for 30 minutes, or until golden. Let stand for 10 minutes. Cut into serving pieces along slits.

Quickbreads and Cookies

Chive Gruyère Biscuits. *128*

Blueberry Lemon Drop Biscuits. *129*

Oatmeal Currant Scones *130*

Cheddar Sage Muffins *131*

Cranberry Banana Muffins. *132*

Apple Bran Muffins. *133*

Blueberry Cinnamon Loaf *134*

Whole Wheat Grain Bread *135*

Monster Potato Hamburger Buns. *136*

Rosemary Garlic Fougasse *138*

Roasted Garlic Bread *140*

Lavender Shortbread *141*

Oatmeal Crisp Cookies. *142*

Date Squares. *143*

Chocolate Chunk Cookie Squares *144*

Chive Gruyère Biscuits

MAKES 10 BISCUITS

Serve these light and flaky savory biscuits with soups, salads or chili.

Make Ahead

Bake biscuits, cool, wrap individually and freeze for up to two weeks. Defrost and reheat at 325°F (160°C) for 10 minutes.

2 cups	all-purpose flour	500 mL
¼ cup	chopped fresh chives or green onions	50 mL
1 tbsp	baking powder	15 mL
½ tsp	salt	2 mL
½ tsp	black pepper	2 mL
½ cup	cold butter, cut in cubes	125 mL
¾ cup	grated Gruyère cheese	175 mL
1 cup	milk, divided	250 mL

1. In a large bowl, combine flour, chives, baking powder, salt and pepper. Using a pastry blender, cut in butter until mixture resembles coarse crumbs. Stir in cheese. Add all but 2 tbsp (25 mL) milk. Stir just until a soft dough forms.

2. Turn dough onto a lightly floured surface. Knead gently, making 8 turns (do not overwork dough). Pat dough down until ½ inch (1 cm) thick.

3. Cut into biscuits with a floured 2½-inch (6 cm) biscuit cutter. Reshape trimmings and cut remaining dough. Place biscuits on a baking sheet. Brush with remaining 2 tbsp (25 mL) milk.

4. Convection bake in a preheated 400°F (200°C) oven for 12 to 14 minutes, or until golden. Serve warm.

Variation

Rosemary Cheddar Biscuits: Use 1 tbsp (15 mL) chopped fresh rosemary instead of chives. Use grated Cheddar cheese instead of Gruyère.

Warm Chèvre Salad with Mexican Pesto (page 106)

Blueberry Lemon Drop Biscuits

MAKES 12 BISCUITS

Drop biscuits eliminate the rolling and cutting process, without forfeiting texture and flavor. Quick to make, these are ideal for breakfast or afternoon tea. If you are using frozen blueberries, add them in the frozen state.

2 cups	all-purpose flour	500 mL
1/4 cup	granulated sugar	50 mL
1 tbsp	grated lemon zest	15 mL
2 tsp	baking powder	10 mL
1/2 tsp	baking soda	2 mL
1/4 tsp	salt	1 mL
1/3 cup	cold butter, cut in cubes	75 mL
1	egg	1
3/4 cup	buttermilk, unflavored yogurt or sour milk (page 131)	175 mL
1 cup	fresh or frozen blueberries	250 mL
TOPPING		
1 tbsp	granulated sugar	15 mL

1. In a large bowl, combine flour, sugar, lemon zest, baking powder, baking soda and salt. Cut in butter until mixture resembles coarse crumbs.
2. In a small bowl, combine egg and buttermilk. Add to flour mixture. Stir just until a soft dough forms. Gently stir in blueberries.
3. Drop mixture by spoonfuls in 12 mounds on a parchment-lined or lightly greased baking sheet. For topping, sprinkle with sugar.
4. Convection bake in a preheated 375°F (190°C) oven for 15 to 18 minutes, or until golden. Cool for a few minutes on wire rack. Serve warm.

Variation
Raspberry Lemon Drop Biscuits: Use fresh or frozen raspberries instead of blueberries.

Oven French Toast with Caramelized Apples (page 115)

Oatmeal Currant Scones

MAKES 8 SERVINGS

Fill the house with fresh-baked aromas first thing in the morning with this easy quickbread. Serve with jams and cheeses.

2 cups	all-purpose flour	500 mL
¼ cup	granulated sugar	50 mL
2 tsp	baking powder	10 mL
½ tsp	baking soda	2 mL
½ tsp	salt	2 mL
½ cup	cold butter, cut in cubes	125 mL
1 cup	rolled oats (not instant)	250 mL
½ cup	currants or golden raisins	125 mL
2 tsp	grated orange zest	10 mL
1	egg	1
¾ cup	buttermilk, unflavored yogurt or sour milk (page 131)	175 mL

TOPPING

2 tbsp	buttermilk	25 mL
1 tbsp	granulated sugar	15 mL

1. In a large bowl, combine flour, sugar, baking powder, baking soda and salt. Cut in butter until mixture resembles coarse crumbs. Stir in rolled oats, currants and orange zest.

2. In a small bowl, combine egg and buttermilk. Add to flour mixture. Stir with a fork until just combined.

3. Turn dough onto a lightly floured surface. Roll dough into a ball and knead gently 8 times. Shape into a 9-inch (23 cm) circle with slightly raised center. Place on a parchment-lined or lightly greased baking sheet.

4. With a sharp knife, score surface with cuts ½-inch (1 cm) deep, making 8 wedges. For topping, brush surface with buttermilk and sprinkle with sugar.

5. Convection bake in a preheated 350°F (180°C) oven for 30 to 35 minutes, or until a tester inserted in center comes out clean. Serve warm.

Variation
Oatmeal Apricot Scones: Use diced dried apricots or cranberries instead of currants.

Cheddar Sage Muffins

MAKES
12 MEDIUM MUFFINS

Include these in
the breakfast or
dinner bread basket.
Use old or extra-old
Cheddar for a
stronger flavor.

Make Ahead
Bake muffins and
cool. Wrap individually
and freeze for up to
three weeks.

2 cups	all-purpose flour	500 mL
1 tsp	baking soda	5 mL
½ tsp	salt	2 mL
2	eggs	2
3 tbsp	granulated sugar	45 mL
⅓ cup	butter, melted	75 mL
1 cup	buttermilk, unflavored yogurt or sour milk	250 mL
1¾ cups	grated Cheddar cheese, divided	425 mL
1 tbsp	chopped fresh sage, or ½ tsp (2 mL) dried	15 mL

1. In a medium bowl, combine flour, baking soda and salt.
2. In a large bowl, mix together eggs, sugar, melted butter and buttermilk. Add flour mixture and stir until just combined. Fold in 1½ cups (375 mL) cheese and sage. Spoon into greased or paper-lined medium muffin cups. Sprinkle remaining ¼ cup (50 mL) cheese over muffin tops.
3. Convection bake in a preheated 350°F (180°C) oven for 15 to 18 minutes, or until tops are firm to touch and golden. Cool in pan for 5 minutes before removing to a wire rack. Serve warm or at room temperature.

> ### Sour Milk
> To sour milk, combine 1 tbsp (15 mL) white vinegar or lemon juice with 1 cup (250 mL) milk. Let stand for 10 minutes before using.

Cranberry Banana Muffins

MAKES
12 MEDIUM MUFFINS

The tang of cranberries is softened by the subtleness of the banana and the hint of nutmeg in this recipe. I always keep a stash of cranberries in the freezer for baking and sauces.

Make Ahead
Bake muffins and cool. Wrap individually and freeze for up to three weeks.

1	ripe banana	1
½ cup	granulated sugar	125 mL
1	egg	1
¾ cup	milk	175 mL
⅓ cup	butter, melted	75 mL
1 tbsp	grated orange zest	15 mL
2 cups	all-purpose flour	500 mL
1 tbsp	baking powder	15 mL
½ tsp	ground nutmeg	2 mL
½ tsp	salt	2 mL
1½ cups	fresh or frozen cranberries	375 mL

1. In a large bowl, mash banana. Add sugar, egg, milk, melted butter and orange zest and combine well.

2. In a medium bowl, combine flour, baking powder, nutmeg and salt. Stir into liquid ingredients until just moistened. Fold in cranberries. Spoon into greased or paper-lined medium muffin cups.

3. Convection bake in a preheated 375°F (190°C) oven for 22 to 25 minutes, or until a tester inserted in center comes out clean. Cool in pan for 5 minutes before removing to wire rack. Serve warm or at room temperature.

Weekend Brunch for 6
Make the scones or muffins ahead of time. Bake the frittata and colcannon in the oven at the same time.

- Fresh Fruit Platter
- Asparagus, Chèvre and Smoked Salmon Frittata (page 118)
- Colcannon Bake (page 97)
- Cold Sliced Ham (page 71)
- Oatmeal Currant Scones (page 130) or Cranberry Banana Muffins (page 132)

Apple Bran Muffins

MAKES
12 MEDIUM MUFFINS

An apple is the secret moistening ingredient in these easy muffins (and you don't even have to peel it).

Make Ahead
Bake muffins and cool. Wrap individually and freeze for up to three weeks.

1 ½ cups	all-purpose flour	375 mL
½ cup	whole wheat flour	125 mL
½ cup	natural bran	125 mL
½ cup	packed brown sugar	125 mL
1 tbsp	baking powder	15 mL
1 tsp	ground cinnamon	5 mL
½ tsp	salt	2 mL
1	egg	1
1 cup	milk	250 mL
¼ cup	vegetable oil	50 mL
2 tbsp	molasses	25 mL
1	apple, cored and grated	1

TOPPING

1 tsp	granulated sugar	5 mL
½ tsp	ground cinnamon	2 mL

1. In a medium bowl, combine all-purpose flour, whole wheat flour, bran, brown sugar, baking powder, cinnamon and salt.

2. In a large bowl, blend together egg, milk, oil, molasses and apple. Stir in flour mixture until just combined. Spoon batter into greased or paper-lined medium muffin cups.

3. For the topping, in a small measuring cup, combine granulated sugar and cinnamon. Sprinkle mixture over top of muffins.

4. Convection bake in a preheated 350°F (180°C) oven for 20 to 22 minutes, or until tops are firm to the touch. Cool in pan for 5 minutes before removing to a wire rack. Serve warm or at room temperature.

Blueberry Cinnamon Loaf

MAKES ONE 8- BY
4-INCH (1.5 L) LOAF

This easy loaf, marbled with blueberries and cinnamon, has a slightly crunchy topping. Take it on picnics, contribute it to bake sales or present it as a hostess gift.

Make Ahead
Loaf can be prepared up to two days before serving. Or bake and cool completely, wrap well and freeze for up to two months. (For convenience, cut loaf into serving pieces, wrap and freeze individually.)

½ cup	butter, softened	125 mL
¾ cup	granulated sugar	175 mL
2	eggs	2
1 tsp	vanilla	5 mL
1 ½ cups	all-purpose flour	375 mL
1 tsp	baking powder	5 mL
½ tsp	baking soda	2 mL
¾ cup	buttermilk, sour milk (page 131) or unflavored yogurt	175 mL
1 cup	fresh or frozen blueberries	250 mL
2 tbsp	packed brown sugar	25 mL
2 tsp	ground cinnamon	10 mL
TOPPING		
1 tbsp	packed brown sugar	25 mL
1 tsp	ground cinnamon	5 mL

1. In a large bowl, beat together butter and granulated sugar until light and fluffy. Beat in eggs one at a time. Beat in vanilla.

2. In a separate bowl, mix together flour, baking powder and baking soda. Add to creamed mixture alternately with buttermilk, making three dry and two liquid additions.

3. In a small bowl, combine blueberries, brown sugar and cinnamon. Gently fold blueberries into batter. Spoon batter into a parchment-lined 8- by 4-inch (1.5 L) loaf pan.

4. For topping, in a small measuring cup, combine brown sugar and cinnamon. Sprinkle topping over loaf. Convection bake in preheated 325°F (160°C) oven for 75 minutes, or until a cake tester inserted in center comes out clean. Let stand for 10 minutes before removing from pan.

Whole Wheat Grain Bread

**MAKES TWO 7-INCH
(18 CM) LOAVES**

A rustic-looking
free-form bread to
serve with cheese, or
to make sandwiches and
toast. The recipe easily
doubles. Eight-grain
cereal is available in bulk
food stores (it is
sometimes called seven-
grain or twelve-grain
cereal). Store it in the
refrigerator or freezer.

Make Ahead
Baked bread can be
cooled, wrapped well and
frozen for up to three
weeks.

2 cups	warm water	500 mL
1 tbsp	active dry yeast (1 package)	15 mL
1 tbsp	liquid honey	15 mL
1 tbsp	vegetable oil	15 mL
1½ tsp	salt	7 mL
½ cup	uncooked eight-grain cereal	125 mL
2 cups	whole wheat flour	500 mL
2 cups	all-purpose flour (approx.)	500 mL

1. In a large bowl, combine water, yeast, honey, oil and salt. Stir and let rest for 5 minutes, or until yeast becomes bubbly.

2. Add cereal, whole wheat flour and 1½ cups (375 mL) all-purpose flour. Stir to combine and form a soft dough. Add more all-purpose flour until dough is too stiff to stir, then turn out onto a floured surface. Knead for 8 minutes, adding enough flour to make a pliable dough. (If you are using an electric mixer fitted with dough hook, knead for about 5 minutes.)

3. Place dough in a lightly oiled bowl, turning to coat dough with oil. Cover bowl with plastic wrap. Let rise in a warm place until doubled, about 1 hour.

4. Deflate dough and knead for 4 minutes. Divide into 2 portions. Shape into round loaves about 6 inches (15 cm) in diameter. Place seam side down on a lightly floured baking sheet. Let rise for 20 minutes.

5. Convection bake in a preheated 400°F (200°C) oven for 20 minutes. Reduce heat to 325°F (160°C) and continue to bake for 15 to 18 minutes, or until loaves are golden brown and sound hollow when tapped. Remove from pan and cool on wire racks.

Monster Potato Hamburger Buns

MAKES
12 LARGE BUNS

For a couple of summers I baked breads, cookies and pies to sell at the local farmer's market. Potato bread was one of the most popular items (it makes great toast!), and now, ten years later, I still bake it for special orders.

When making a potato dough, it seems as if you could keep adding flour forever. However, try not to add much more than 4½ cups (1.125 L); the dough should still be slightly sticky. Use older or baking potatoes that mash well.

Make Ahead
Both buns and bread freeze well. Cool completely, package and freeze for up to three weeks.

1 lb	potatoes, peeled	500 g
1 tbsp	active dry yeast (1 package)	15 mL
6 tsp	granulated sugar, divided	30 mL
2 tbsp	olive oil	25 mL
2 tsp	salt	10 mL
4½ cups	all-purpose flour (approx.)	1.125 L

1. In a saucepan, cover potatoes with cold salted water. Bring to a boil and cook for 25 minutes, or until tender. Drain well, reserving 1¾ cups (425 mL) potato-cooking water.

2. Mash potatoes well (but don't worry if there are still lumps). Cool potatoes and potato-cooking water until warm.

3. In a large bowl, combine yeast, 1 tsp (5 mL) sugar and warm potato water. Let stand for 10 minutes or until mixture is foamy.

4. Stir in mashed potatoes, olive oil, remaining 5 tsp (25 mL) sugar, salt and 3½ cups (875 mL) flour to make a sticky dough. Stir in additional flour until dough is too stiff to stir.

5. Turn dough onto a floured surface. Knead, adding enough flour to make a pliable dough (dough may be slightly sticky), about 10 minutes. (If you are using an electric mixer fitted with dough hook, knead for about 5 minutes.)

6. Shape dough into a ball and place in a lightly oiled bowl. Turn dough to coat with oil. Cover bowl with plastic wrap. Let dough rise for 1¼ to 1½ hours or until doubled.

7. Deflate dough and turn out onto a floured surface. Roll roughly into a rope. Divide into 12 pieces.

8. Shape each piece into a round flattened bun about 4 inches (10 cm) in diameter. Place on two flour-dusted baking sheets. Dust tops with flour. Let rise for 15 minutes, then flatten slightly. Let rise for 20 minutes longer.

9. Convection bake in a preheated 375°F (190°C) oven for 22 to 25 minutes, or until golden. Cool on wire racks.

Variation

Potato Bread: In Step 7, divide dough into two equal portions and shape into loaves. Place in two lightly greased 8- by 4-inch (1.5 L) or 9- by 5-inch (2 L) loaf pans. Dust lightly with flour. Let rise until doubled, about 45 minutes. Bake for 35 to 40 minutes, or until bottom sounds hollow when removed from pan. Cool completely on racks.

Apple Butter

Place 5 peeled, cored and chopped apples in a saucepan with $\frac{1}{4}$ cup (50 mL) water, 3 tbsp (45 mL) packed brown sugar, $\frac{1}{4}$ cup (50 mL) butter, 1 tsp (5 mL) cinnamon and 1 tsp (5 mL) grated lemon zest. Bring to a boil. Cover and reduce heat to low. Cook for 10 to 15 minutes, or until apples are softened. Puree or mash until smooth. Serve warm or refrigerate, covered, for up to a week. Makes about 2 cups (500 mL).

Quick Berry Jam

In a medium saucepan, combine 2 cups (500 mL) fresh or frozen raspberries or blueberries, $\frac{1}{3}$ cup (75 mL) liquid honey or granulated sugar and 2 tbsp (25 mL) lemon juice. Bring to a boil, stirring often. Reduce heat to medium-low and cook, uncovered, for 12 to 15 minutes, or until thickened, stirring often. Cool to room temperature before serving or cover and refrigerate for up to a week. Makes about $1\frac{1}{2}$ cups (375 mL).

Rosemary Garlic Fougasse

MAKES 1 FOUGASSE

While working with Lydie Marshall at her cooking school in Nyons, France, we made many variations of fougasse. This oval Provençal flatbread has slits cut into it to give a leaf-like appearance. Some are simply brushed with olive oil and sprinkled with coarse salt. Others may be flavored with coarsely chopped pitted olives or herbes de Provence (page 23).

This is best served the same day it is made. Serve as a light meal with Quick Tomatoes Provençal, olives and cheese.

1 cup	warm water, divided	250 mL
1 tsp	granulated sugar	5 mL
1 tbsp	active dry yeast (1 package)	15 mL
½ cup	warm milk	125 mL
¼ cup	olive oil, divided	50 mL
2 tbsp	chopped fresh rosemary	25 mL
1 tbsp	finely chopped garlic	15 mL
2 tsp	salt	10 mL
3¼ cups	all-purpose flour (approx.)	800 mL
1 tsp	coarse salt	5 mL

1. In a small bowl, combine ½ cup (125 mL) warm water and sugar. Sprinkle yeast over top. Let rise until foamy, about 10 minutes.

2. In a large bowl, combine remaining ½ cup (125 mL) warm water, warm milk, 2 tbsp (25 mL) olive oil, rosemary, garlic and salt.

3. Stir down yeast and add to rosemary mixture. Add 2½ cups (625 mL) flour, stirring to combine. Stir in enough additional flour to make a soft dough.

4. Turn out onto a floured surface and knead for 8 minutes, adding just enough flour to keep dough from sticking. Place in large, lightly oiled bowl, turning dough to coat with oil. Cover bowl with plastic wrap and let rise until doubled in volume, about 1 hour.

5. Deflate dough. Roll into an oval about 14 by 10 inches (36 by 25 cm). Place on an oiled baking sheet.

6. Using a sharp knife or kitchen shears, cut several slashes in dough. Brush with remaining 2 tbsp (25 mL) olive oil and sprinkle with coarse salt. Let rise for 45 to 60 minutes, or until doubled in volume.

7. Convection bake in a preheated 400°F (200°C) oven for 15 to 18 minutes, or until golden. Remove from oven and slide onto a rack. Serve warm or at room temperature.

Yeast

Dry yeast is available in both packages and cans. The yeast recipes in this book are written for packaged active dry yeast. When purchasing yeast, check the expiry date to ensure freshness.

Quick Tomatoes Provençal

Slice 4 tomatoes in half crosswise and place cut side up on a baking sheet. In a small bowl, combine 2 minced cloves garlic, 2 tbsp (25 mL) fresh bread crumbs, 1 tsp (5 mL) herbes de Provence (page 23), ¼ tsp (1 mL) salt and ¼ tsp (1 mL) black pepper. Sprinkle over tomatoes. Drizzle with 2 tbsp (25 mL) olive oil. Place 4 inches (10 cm) from heat and convection broil for 4 to 5 minutes, until topping is golden and tomatoes are slightly soft. Makes 3 to 4 servings.

Roasted Garlic Bread

**MAKES 8
TO 10 SERVINGS**

Roasted garlic, herbs and cheese highlight a simple loaf of crusty bread. This is a good accompaniment for soups, salads and luncheon dishes.

When roasting garlic, roast several heads. Cool the extras, wrap individually and freeze. Use later to top up the flavor of spreads, soups and sauces.

Make Ahead

Garlic can be roasted, wrapped and refrigerated up to three days ahead or frozen for up to six weeks. Bring garlic to room temperature so it is easier to squeeze out of the skin. The garlic sauce can be covered and refrigerated up to a day ahead or frozen for up to two weeks.

3	heads garlic	3
5 tbsp	olive oil, divided	65 mL
1/4 cup	chopped fresh parsley	50 mL
2 tbsp	chopped fresh oregano, or 1 tsp (5 mL) dried	25 mL
1/2 tsp	salt	2 mL
1/4 tsp	black pepper	1 mL
1	loaf French or Italian bread, cut in 1/2-inch (1 cm) slices	1
1/4 cup	grated Parmesan cheese	50 mL

1. To roast garlic, cut tops off heads to expose cloves. Pour 1 tbsp (15 mL) olive oil into a small parchment-lined baking dish. Swirl garlic in oil, cut side down, to coat surface.

2. Convection bake or roast in a 350°F (180°C) oven for 35 minutes, or until garlic is soft when squeezed. When cool enough to handle, squeeze cloves into a small bowl and mash.

3. Add remaining 1/4 cup (50 mL) olive oil, parsley, oregano, salt and pepper to bowl and combine well.

4. Arrange bread slices on two parchment-lined baking sheets. Convection bake in a preheated 350°F (180°C) oven for 5 minutes. Turn bread slices. Spread with garlic mixture and sprinkle with Parmesan. Bake for 8 to 10 minutes, or until hot and lightly toasted.

Lavender Shortbread

MAKES ABOUT
6½ DOZEN

December marks a flurry of baking activity. Baking for cookie exchanges, school or office functions, hostess gifts and home entertaining can be overwhelming, but shortbread is so easy, and the lavender makes this version a bit different.

Look for organic lavender at specialty food shops or grow and dry your own. Or try the excellent variation using lemon and rosemary.

For hostess gifts or cookie exchanges, package cookies in small plastic or cellophane bags. Tie with colored ribbons and hand-printed labels. (I often make up the packages before freezing so they are ready to go when needed.)

Make Ahead
Layer cooled cookies between sheets of waxed paper in an airtight container. Store at room temperature for up to two days or freeze for up to three weeks.

2 cups	butter, softened	500 mL
1 cup	granulated sugar	250 mL
3 cups	all-purpose flour	750 mL
½ cup	rice flour	125 mL
½ cup	cornstarch	125 mL
4 tsp	fresh or dried organic lavender buds	20 mL
¼ cup	confectioner's (icing) sugar, sifted	50 mL

1. In a large bowl, cream together butter and sugar until light and fluffy. In a separate bowl, mix together all-purpose flour, rice flour, cornstarch and lavender. Add to butter mixture and stir until blended. Refrigerate for 30 to 60 minutes, or until firm enough to roll.

2. Roll dough into 1-inch (2.5 cm) balls. Place on parchment-lined baking sheets about 1 inch (2.5 cm) apart. Dip a cookie press in granulated sugar and press dough lightly to make an imprint.

3. Convection bake in a preheated 300°F (150°C) oven for 22 to 25 minutes, or until cookies are just firm to touch and slightly golden. Cool completely. Dust with icing sugar.

Variation
Lemon Rosemary Shortbread: Omit lavender. Add 1 tbsp (15 mL) grated lemon zest and 1 tbsp (15 mL) chopped fresh rosemary.

Classic Shortbread: Omit lavender.

Oatmeal Crisp Cookies

MAKES ABOUT
6 DOZEN

When the newspaper that I write for moved office, I made these cookies for the editors and staff to celebrate the move. The convection oven is perfect for these crisp cookies, which have a great shelf life, if they last that long! Sometimes I place a small scoop of ice cream between two cookies, wrap and freeze to make ice-cream sandwiches.

Make Ahead

Cookies can be stored in an airtight container for up to a week at room temperature, or packaged well frozen for up to three weeks.

1 cup	butter, softened	250 mL
3/4 cup	packed brown sugar	175 mL
1 cup	granulated sugar, divided	250 mL
2	eggs	2
1 tsp	vanilla	5 mL
2 1/2 cups	rolled oats (not instant)	625 mL
1 1/2 cups	all-purpose flour	375 mL
1 cup	unsweetened shredded coconut	250 mL
1/2 tsp	salt	2 mL
1/2 tsp	baking soda	2 mL
1/2 tsp	ground cinnamon	2 mL

1. In a large bowl, cream together butter, brown sugar and 1/2 cup (125 mL) granulated sugar until light and fluffy. Add eggs one at a time, beating until well incorporated. Beat in vanilla.

2. In a separate bowl, combine rolled oats, flour, coconut, salt, baking soda and cinnamon. Add to creamed mixture and mix until all ingredients are incorporated, but do not overmix. Refrigerate dough for 3 hours or until it can be easily shaped by hand.

3. Place remaining 1/2 cup (125 mL) granulated sugar in a shallow dish. Form dough into 1-inch (2.5 cm) balls and place in dish. Roll dough to coat with sugar.

4. Arrange cookies on parchment-lined baking sheets, about 2 inches (5 cm) apart. With a fork dipped in granulated sugar, press cookies to flatten to 1/4-inch (5 mm) thickness.

5. Convection bake in a preheated 350°F (180°C) oven, in batches, for 10 to 12 minutes, or until firm and golden. Transfer to racks to cool.

Date Squares

MAKES 25 SQUARES

An old-fashioned favorite of date filling tucked between layers of tasty oatmeal. Lemon juice and zest cut the sweetness of the dates. For bake sales or easier freezing, cut the whole pan into four large squares. (Some of my customers would treat the large square as one piece!)

Make Ahead
Squares can be covered and stored at room temperature for two days or frozen for up to a month.

2½ cups	pitted dates	625 mL
3 tbsp	lemon juice	45 mL
2 tsp	grated lemon zest	10 mL
Pinch	salt	Pinch
1½ cups	water	375 mL
1½ cups	all-purpose flour	375 mL
1 cup	packed brown sugar	250 mL
½ tsp	baking powder	2 mL
¾ cup	cold butter, cut in cubes	175 mL
1½ cups	rolled oats (not instant)	375 mL

1. To prepare filling, in a medium saucepan, combine dates, lemon juice, zest, salt and water. Bring to a boil. Reduce heat to medium and simmer for 12 minutes, or until mixture is thick. Stir frequently to break up dates. Cool completely.

2. In a large bowl, combine flour, sugar and baking powder. Cut in butter until mixture resembles coarse crumbs. Stir in oatmeal and cut in slightly.

3. Pat two-thirds of crumb mixture into a lightly greased and parchment-lined 9-inch (2.5 L) square baking pan. Spread date filling over top. Spread with remaining crumb mixture and pat down lightly.

4. Convection bake in a preheated 325°F (160°C) oven for 35 minutes, or until golden brown. Cool completely on rack. Lift out before cutting into small squares.

Chocolate Chunk Cookie Squares

MAKES 25 SQUARES

Square chocolate chip cookies! I like to use Swiss milk chocolate with honey and almonds in these cookies, but semisweet or bittersweet chocolate can also be used.

When baking squares, line the pan with parchment so the paper extends ¾ inch (2 cm) over two sides, then grease paper. The paper acts as a handle to lift the squares out of the pan completely before cutting. (Be sure to loosen the other sides with a knife.)

Make Ahead
Squares can be baked, covered and refrigerated for up to two days or frozen for up to a month.

⅓ cup	butter, softened	75 mL
⅓ cup	shortening, softened	75 mL
½ cup	packed brown sugar	125 mL
½ cup	granulated sugar	125 mL
2	eggs	2
1¾ cups	all-purpose flour	425 mL
1½ tsp	baking powder	7 mL
½ tsp	salt	2 mL
2½ cups	coarsely chopped chocolate (about 12 oz/375 g), divided	625 mL
½ cup	chopped pecans (optional)	125 mL

1. In a large bowl, cream together butter, shortening and both sugars until light. Beat in eggs one at a time.

2. In a separate bowl, combine flour, baking powder and salt. Stir into creamed mixture and blend well. Gently stir in 2 cups (500 mL) chocolate chunks and pecans, if using. Spread batter evenly over lightly greased and parchment-lined 9-inch (2.5 L) square baking dish. Sprinkle remaining ½ cup (125 mL) chocolate over surface.

3. Convection bake in a preheated 325°F (160°C) oven for 35 minutes, or until squares are golden brown and firm to touch.

4. Cool completely in pan on rack. Lift out of pan before cutting into squares.

Weeknight Dinner for 5 to 6
The cookie squares can be made ahead or cooked at the same time as the tortellini. For a simple raw vegetable salad, toss sliced cucumber, broccoli florets, sliced red bell pepper and grated carrot with your favorite salad dressing or vinaigrette.

- Tortellini Casserole (page 84)
- Raw Vegetable Salad
- Chocolate Chunk Cookie Squares (page 144)

Desserts

Rhubarb Coffee Cake *146*

Ginger Gingerbread *147*

Carrot Cake. *148*

Peach Upside-down Cake. *149*

Almond Angel Cake *150*

Strawberry Rhubarb Crunch *151*

Lemon and White Chocolate Napoleons *152*

Apple Cranberry Strudel. *154*

Chocolate Almond Torte. *155*

Apple Pie with Cheddar Pastry. *156*

Bonnie Stern's Pavlova *158*

Chocolate Bread Pudding
with Chocolate Bourbon Sauce *159*

Pumpkin Praline Pie. *160*

Open-face Apricot Tart. *162*

Rhubarb Coffee Cake

MAKES ONE
9-INCH (23 CM)
SQUARE CAKE

This cake is great even without the crunchy topping. Serve it for brunch, or with coffee or tea, accompanied by fresh strawberries or other seasonal fruit.

Make Ahead

Cake can be stored in an airtight container at room temperature for up to a day. To freeze, wrap in plastic wrap, then wrap in foil and freeze for up to two weeks.

TOPPING		
¾ cup	packed brown sugar	175 mL
½ cup	chopped pecans or almonds	125 mL
2 tsp	ground cinnamon	10 mL
2 tbsp	butter, melted	25 mL
CAKE		
½ cup	butter, softened	125 mL
¾ cup	granulated sugar	175 mL
1	egg	1
2 tsp	grated orange zest	10 mL
1 tsp	vanilla	5 mL
2 cups	all-purpose flour	500 mL
1 tsp	baking soda	5 mL
½ tsp	salt	2 mL
1 cup	unflavored yogurt or buttermilk	250 mL
2 cups	diced fresh or frozen rhubarb	500 mL

1. To prepare topping, in a small bowl, combine brown sugar, pecans, cinnamon and melted butter.

2. To make cake, in a large bowl, cream softened butter and granulated sugar together until light. Beat in egg, orange zest and vanilla.

3. In a separate bowl, combine flour, baking soda and salt. Stir into creamed mixture alternately with yogurt, making three additions of dry ingredients and two of yogurt. Stir in rhubarb. Spread batter in a parchment-lined or greased 9-inch (2 L) square baking pan. Sprinkle topping over cake.

4. Convection bake in a preheated 325°F (160°C) oven for 45 to 50 minutes, or until a cake tester inserted in center comes out clean. Let cool in pan on a rack.

Variations

Blueberry Coffee Cake: Use fresh or frozen blueberries instead of rhubarb.

Apple Coffee Cake: Use diced apple instead of rhubarb.

Ginger Gingerbread

MAKES ONE
8-INCH (20 CM)
SQUARE CAKE

Candied ginger adds extra flavor to this old-fashioned cake. Serve it with pear sauce or apple sauce or cut into smaller pieces for tea time.

Make Ahead

Gingerbread can be wrapped well and frozen for up to three weeks. You can also cut the cake into individual pieces and wrap separately before freezing.

1 ½ cups	all-purpose flour	375 mL
¾ tsp	baking powder	4 mL
½ tsp	baking soda	2 mL
½ tsp	salt	2 mL
1 tsp	ground ginger	5 mL
½ tsp	ground cinnamon	2 mL
¼ tsp	ground nutmeg	1 mL
3 tbsp	chopped candied ginger	45 mL
½ cup	sour cream or buttermilk	125 mL
¼ cup	molasses	50 mL
½ cup	butter, softened	125 mL
½ cup	packed brown sugar	125 mL
2	eggs	2

1. In a medium bowl, combine flour, baking powder, baking soda, salt, ground ginger, cinnamon, nutmeg and candied ginger. Combine well.

2. In a measuring cup, mix together sour cream and molasses.

3. In a large bowl, beat together butter and sugar until light. Beat in eggs one at a time. Add dry and liquid ingredients alternately, making three dry and two liquid additions. Spread mixture in a greased 8-inch (2 L) square baking dish.

4. Convection bake in a preheated 325°F (160°C) oven for 40 to 45 minutes, or until a cake tester inserted in center comes out clean. Cool in pan for 15 minutes before turning out onto wire rack to cool completely.

Asian-flavored Dinner for 6
Make the quesadillas and dessert ahead of time.

- Chicken Satay Quesadillas (page 26)
- Fish Fillets with Miso Dressing (page 42)
- Stir-fried Rice (page 175)
- Ginger Gingerbread (page 147) or Bonnie Stern's Pavlova (page 158)

Carrot Cake

MAKES ONE
9-INCH (23 CM)
ROUND CAKE

For several years I baked desserts and breads for an inn, and this cake flew out of the kitchen. It has also made appearances at weddings, birthdays and picnics. Since convection cooking allows cooking on several racks, make at least three cakes at a time and freeze.

Make Ahead
Cake can be prepared, covered and refrigerated for two days with or without icing. Un-iced cake can be wrapped well and frozen for up to a month.

3	eggs	3
2 cups	grated carrots	500 mL
1 cup	packed brown sugar	250 mL
½ cup	golden raisins	125 mL
½ cup	vegetable oil	125 mL
1½ cups	all-purpose flour	375 mL
1 tsp	baking powder	5 mL
¾ tsp	baking soda	4 mL
1 tsp	ground cinnamon	5 mL
½ tsp	ground allspice	2 mL
½ tsp	salt	2 mL

CREAM CHEESE ICING

8 oz	cream cheese, softened	250 g
¼ cup	butter, softened	50 mL
1 cup	confectioner's (icing) sugar	250 mL
1 tsp	grated orange zest	5 mL

1. In a large bowl, combine eggs, carrots, brown sugar, raisins and oil. Mix thoroughly.

2. In a separate bowl, stir together flour, baking powder, baking soda, cinnamon, allspice and salt. Add dry ingredients to carrot mixture and stir to combine. Spread in a greased 9-inch (23 cm) round cake pan with 2-inch (5 cm) sides.

3. Convection bake in a preheated 325°F (160°C) oven for 30 minutes, or until a cake tester inserted in center comes out clean. Cool in pan for 5 minutes. Turn out onto a wire rack and cool completely.

4. Meanwhile, to prepare icing, in a large bowl, blend together cream cheese and butter until smooth. Gradually sift in icing sugar and combine well. Stir in orange zest.

5. Place cake on a serving plate and spread icing over top and sides. Refrigerate to firm icing.

Peach Upside-down Cake

**MAKES ONE
9-INCH (23 CM)
SQUARE CAKE**

Celebrate the start of peach season with this irresistible cake. (Other fresh fruits such as plums, raspberries, rhubarb, nectarines and cranberries could also be used.) Serve this the same day it is baked for brunch, dessert or picnics.

1/3 cup	butter, melted	75 mL
3/4 cup	packed brown sugar	175 mL
1 1/2 cups	peeled, sliced peaches (about 5)	375 mL
1/2 cup	butter, softened	125 mL
2/3 cup	granulated sugar	175 mL
2	eggs	2
1/2 tsp	almond extract or vanilla	2 mL
1 1/2 cups	all-purpose flour	375 mL
1 1/2 tsp	baking powder	7 mL
1/2 tsp	baking soda	2 mL
1/4 tsp	salt	1 mL
3/4 cup	buttermilk or unflavored yogurt	175 mL

1. Pour melted butter into a 9-inch (2 L) square baking pan. Swirl butter up sides. Sprinkle brown sugar over bottom of pan. Arrange peach slices over sugar.

2. In a large bowl, cream together butter and granulated sugar until light. Add eggs one at a time. Beat in almond extract.

3. In a separate bowl, combine flour, baking powder, baking soda and salt. Add flour mixture and buttermilk alternately to egg mixture, making three dry additions and two liquid. Spread batter over peaches.

4. Convection bake in a preheated 325°F (160°C) oven for 45 minutes, or until a cake tester inserted in center comes out clean. Cool cake in pan on a rack for 15 minutes. Run knife around edge of pan and invert cake onto serving plate. Serve warm or at room temperature.

Casual Dinner for 4 to 6
Make the Caesar salad ahead. Cook the cake at the same time as the chicken.

- Raw Vegetables with Savory Dip (page 30)
- Potato and Bean Caesar Salad (page 105)
- Roasted Flat Chicken (page 46)
- Peach Upside-down Cake (page 149)

Almond Angel Cake

MAKES ONE
10-INCH (25 CM)
CAKE

This is the very first cake I ever made. It is my mother's recipe and I first made it when I was nine (for special occasions, we would ice it with fluffy frosting).

Angel cake has recently regained popularity as a lower-fat dessert. Serve it with fresh fruit or lemon mousse (page 152).

Make Ahead
Store in an airtight container at room temperature for up to two days or wrap well and freeze for up to a month.

1 1/2 cups	granulated sugar, divided	375 mL
1 cup	cake flour	250 mL
1 1/2 cups	egg whites (about 12 eggs), at room temperature	375 mL
1 tsp	cream of tartar	5 mL
1/2 tsp	salt	2 mL
1 tsp	almond extract	5 mL
1/2 tsp	vanilla	2 mL

1. In a bowl, sift together ¾ cup (175 mL) sugar and flour. Sift again.

2. In a large clean bowl, combine egg whites with cream of tartar and salt. Beat egg whites until soft peaks form. Gradually add remaining ¾ cup (175 mL) sugar, beating until egg whites are firm. Beat in almond extract and vanilla.

3. Sift one-third of flour mixture over egg whites and fold in gently. Repeat twice with remaining flour, folding in carefully after each addition. Spoon mixture into an ungreased 10-inch (4 L) tube pan. Run knife gently through batter to release any large air bubbles. Smooth surface lightly.

4. Convection bake in a preheated 325°F (160°C) oven for 40 to 45 minutes, or until cake is firm to the touch. Remove from oven. Invert pan. Cool completely before removing from pan.

Variation
Mocha Chocolate Chip Angel Cake: Add 1 tbsp (15 mL) crushed instant coffee powder to flour mixture. Omit almond extract. Fold 1 cup (250 mL) chocolate chips into cake after last flour addition. Serve with Chocolate Bourbon Sauce (page 159).

Strawberry Rhubarb Crunch

MAKES 5
TO 6 SERVINGS

The tangy sweet combination of strawberry and rhubarb appears in compotes, pies, jams and desserts. Flour has purposely been omitted from the base so the filling will be juicy (the crunch topping will absorb the juices on standing). However, if you are using frozen fruit, add 2 tbsp (25 mL) flour to the fruit.

Make Ahead
Topping can be prepared up to eight hours ahead, but do not taste it or you will need to make it again!

3 ½ cups	sliced fresh or frozen rhubarb	875 mL
3 cups	sliced fresh or frozen strawberries	750 mL
½ cup	granulated sugar	125 mL
TOPPING		
¼ cup	butter	50 mL
¼ cup	liquid honey	50 mL
1 cup	rolled oats (not instant)	250 mL
½ cup	all-purpose flour	125 mL
½ cup	chopped hazelnuts or pecans	125 mL
¼ cup	packed brown sugar	50 mL
¼ tsp	ground nutmeg	1 mL

1. In an 8-inch (2 L) square baking dish, combine rhubarb and strawberries. Sprinkle fruit with granulated sugar and combine with a fork.

2. In a small saucepan, combine butter and honey. Heat over low heat for a few minutes until melted and combined.

3. In a large bowl, combine rolled oats, flour, nuts, brown sugar and nutmeg. Add butter mixture and combine to moisten ingredients. Spread crumb mixture over fruit.

4. Convection bake in a preheated 350°F (180°C) oven for 35 minutes, or until rhubarb is tender. (If crunch is browning too much near end of cooking time, cover loosely with foil.) Let stand for 30 minutes before serving.

Lemon and
White Chocolate Napoleons

MAKES 8 SERVINGS

Lemon combined with white chocolate creates a smooth, luscious filling for puff pastry. A small amount of gelatin helps prevent the mousse from "sinking." For a shortcake effect, spoon on sliced strawberries or other fresh berries before adding the top pastry.

Make Ahead

Puff pastry can be baked and stored in an airtight container for one day. Mousse can be covered and refrigerated a day in advance.

PASTRY

1	14-oz (397 g) package frozen puff pastry, defrosted	1
1	egg yolk	1
1 tbsp	milk	15 mL
2 tsp	granulated sugar	10 mL

LEMON AND WHITE CHOCOLATE MOUSSE

½	package unflavored gelatin (about 1½ tsp/7 mL)	½
¼ cup	cold water	50 mL
¾ cup	granulated sugar	175 mL
2 tbsp	grated lemon zest	25 mL
½ cup	lemon juice	125 mL
3	egg yolks	3
4 oz	white chocolate, chopped (about 1 cup/250 mL)	125 g
1½ cups	whipping (35%) cream	375 mL
2 tbsp	confectioner's (icing) sugar	25 mL
2½ cups	fresh fruit (strawberries, raspberries, sliced peaches or blueberries)	625 mL

1. To prepare pastry, on a lightly floured surface, roll out half of pastry into an 8-inch (20 cm) square. Cut into four 4-inch (10 cm) squares (I use a ravioli cutter for a crinkled edge). Place on a parchment-lined baking sheet. Repeat with remaining dough.

2. In a small bowl, beat together egg yolk and milk. Brush over pastry. Sprinkle with sugar. Pierce each piece of pastry several times with a fork.

3. Convection bake or roast in a preheated 375°F (190°C) oven for 15 minutes, or until golden brown. Turn baking sheets after 10 minutes if pastry is browning too much. Cool on wire racks.

4. Meanwhile, to prepare mousse, sprinkle gelatin over cold water in a small saucepan to soften. Heat over low heat for about 3 minutes to dissolve.

5. In a medium saucepan, whisk together granulated sugar, lemon zest, lemon juice and egg yolks. Place over medium heat and bring slowly to a boil, whisking constantly. Cook for 3 minutes until just thickened. Remove from heat. Stir in gelatin and chocolate until dissolved, about 1 minute.

6. Transfer mousse to a large bowl and refrigerate just until cool, about 30 minutes. (To cool mousse more quickly, place in a stainless-steel bowl set over ice water. Stir occasionally. Fold in whipped cream before filling sets completely.)

7. In a large bowl, whip cream until soft peaks form. Fold into lemon mixture. Cover and refrigerate until serving time.

8. To assemble, cut pastries in half. Place one half on each serving plate. Spoon one-eighth of mousse mixture over bottom pastry. Place pastry top over mousse. Sift icing sugar over top and garnish with fresh fruit.

Apple Cranberry Strudel

MAKES 8 SERVINGS

Phyllo pastry simplifies the strudel-making process, and it cooks beautifully in the convection oven. Use apples that hold their shape well, such as Northern Spy, Golden Delicious or Ida Red. Strudel is best served the same day it is baked. Serve with vanilla ice cream.

For easier cleanup, line the baking sheet with both foil and parchment-paper, as the apple juices tend to run and burn onto the pan.

4	large apples, peeled and sliced	4
½ cup	dried cranberries	125 mL
⅓ cup	granulated sugar	75 mL
¼ cup	chopped pecans	50 mL
1 tsp	grated lemon zest	5 mL
½ tsp	ground cinnamon	2 mL
6	sheets phyllo pastry	6
¼ cup	butter, melted (approx.)	50 mL
⅓ cup	dry bread crumbs	75 mL

1. In a large bowl, combine apples, cranberries, sugar, pecans, lemon zest and cinnamon.

2. Place a sheet of phyllo pastry on a flat surface. Brush lightly with melted butter and sprinkle with approx. 1 tbsp (15 mL) bread crumbs. Place a second sheet of phyllo on top of first. Brush with butter and sprinkle with bread crumbs. Continue to layer phyllo, butter and crumbs.

3. Spoon apple mixture lengthwise along pastry about 2 inches (5 cm) from long edge. Roll up pastry to enclose apples. Carefully place strudel, seam side down, on a foil- *and* parchment-lined baking sheet. Tuck in any escaping apples. With a serrated knife, make 7 cuts through top of pastry to mark 8 servings. Brush top with melted butter.

4. Convection bake or roast in a preheated 350°F (180°C) oven for 35 minutes, or until apples are tender and pastry is golden. Cool in pan on a wire rack. Serve warm.

Edible Flowers

Edible flowers include roses, marigolds, nasturtiums, pansies, borage and daisies. Make sure the flowers have been organically grown (pesticide free), or grow your own.

Chocolate Almond Torte

MAKES ONE 8-INCH
(20 CM) TORTE

This flourless torte is
small, but it is dense
and rich and will satisfy
any chocolate lover. It
can be served without the
glaze (just dust with icing
sugar or add a dollop of
whipped cream), but the
chocolate glaze does add
a sleek, finishing touch.

The chocolate can be
melted in a microwave
on Medium heat. Watch
it carefully. Remove the
chocolate from the oven
just when it collapses
and stir until completely
melted. For the best
flavor and texture, grind
the almonds yourself
in a food processor or
with a rotary hand grater
rather than buying
preground almonds.

Make Ahead
Torte can be glazed,
covered and refrigerated
for up to two days or
frozen, unglazed, for
up to six weeks.

½ cup	butter, softened	125 mL
⅔ cup	granulated sugar	150 mL
3	eggs	3
4 oz	semisweet or bittersweet chocolate, melted and slightly cooled	125 g
1 ¼ cups	ground almonds	300 mL
1 tsp	grated orange zest	5 mL
GLAZE		
4 oz	semisweet or bittersweet chocolate, chopped (about 1 cup/250 mL)	125 g
¼ cup	whipping (35%) cream	50 mL
1 tbsp	orange liqueur	15 mL

1. To prepare cake, cream butter and sugar in a large
   bowl. Beat in eggs one at a time. Slowly beat in melted
   chocolate. Stir in almonds and orange zest. Turn mixture
   into a lightly greased *and* parchment-lined 8-inch
   (20 cm) round cake pan.

2. Convection bake in a preheated 350°F (180°C) oven
   for 25 to 28 minutes, or until a skewer inserted in center
   comes out almost clean (cake may appear a bit soft in
   center). Cool in pan on a rack for 30 minutes. Run
   knife around edge of cake. Invert and cool completely.

3. To prepare glaze, place chopped chocolate and cream in
   a stainless-steel bowl set over hot water. Melt and stir
   together. Remove from heat and add liqueur. Cool glaze
   until thick enough to spread (to speed up this process,
   place over bowl of ice water and stir).

4. Place cake on a serving plate. Pour glaze over cake,
   letting it run down sides.

Apple Pie
with Cheddar Pastry

MAKES ONE
9-INCH (23 CM) PIE

A variation on an old favorite. Serve with a dollop of whipped cream or yogurt cheese (page 158). The added Cheddar results in a crusty pastry. I often use this pastry for meat or chicken pies, too.

CHEDDAR PASTRY

1 ½ cups	all-purpose flour	375 mL
½ cup	grated Cheddar cheese	125 mL
½ tsp	salt	2 mL
¼ cup	cold butter, cut in pieces	50 mL
¼ cup	cold lard or shortening, cut in pieces	50 mL
5 tbsp	ice-cold water (approx.)	65 mL

FILLING

6	apples (Northern Spy, Ida Red, Golden Delicious), peeled and sliced	6
⅓ cup	granulated sugar	75 mL
2 tbsp	all-purpose flour	25 mL
1 tbsp	lemon juice	15 mL
1 tbsp	cold butter, cut in bits	15 mL

TOPPING

⅓ cup	all-purpose flour	75 mL
⅓ cup	packed brown sugar	75 mL
½ cup	grated Cheddar cheese	125 mL
1 tsp	ground cinnamon	5 mL
¼ cup	cold butter, cut in pieces	50 mL

1. To prepare pastry, combine flour, cheese and salt in a large bowl. Using a pastry blender or two knives, cut in butter and lard until mixture resembles coarse crumbs with a few larger pieces. Drizzle ice water over dry ingredients, stirring with a fork until a rough dough forms. Bring dough together and shape into a disc. Wrap in plastic and refrigerate for 20 minutes.

2. Roll out dough on a lightly floured surface to an 11-inch (28 cm) circle. Ease into a 9-inch (23 cm) pie plate. Fold overhang under at rim. Flute edge.

3. For the filling, in a large bowl, combine apples, granulated sugar, flour, lemon juice and butter. Combine thoroughly. Turn into prepared pie shell, mounding apples in center.

4. For the topping, in a small bowl, combine flour, brown sugar, cheese and cinnamon. Cut in butter until it is in tiny bits. Sprinkle topping over apples.

5. Convection bake or roast in a preheated 400°F (200°C) oven for 15 minutes. Reduce heat to 325°F (160°C) and continue to bake for 45 to 50 minutes, or until apples test tender. Cool on a rack.

Variation
Cheddar Cheese Sticks: Roll out Cheddar pastry and cut into circles or thin sticks. Convection bake in a preheated 400°F (200°C) oven for 8 to 10 minutes, or until golden brown. Serve with soups or salads.

Bonnie Stern's Pavlova

MAKES 8 SERVINGS

This is one of the great HeartSmart dessert recipes from Bonnie Stern, owner of her own cooking school in Toronto and the author of ten delicious cookbooks. The convection oven is fabulous for cooking meringues because of its continuous circulating heat.

Garnish with edible flowers (page 154).

4	egg whites	4
1 cup	granulated sugar	250 mL
2 tsp	white vinegar	10 mL
1 ½ cups	yogurt cheese	375 mL
2 tbsp	liquid honey or confectioner's (icing) sugar	25 mL
1 tsp	vanilla	5 mL
4 cups	fresh blueberries, raspberries or strawberries, or a combination	1 L

1. In a large, very clean bowl, beat egg whites until light.
2. Gradually add granulated sugar to egg whites and beat until firm. Beat in vinegar.
3. Outline a 10-inch (25 cm) circle on a piece of parchment paper and place on a baking sheet. Spoon egg whites inside circle and spread in loose waves.
4. Convection bake in a preheated 250°F (120°C) oven for 2 hours. Remove from oven and cool. (If kitchen is very humid, store pavlova in a dry place such as a turned-off oven; leave a note on the oven door so you don't forget it's in there!)
5. For the filling, combine yogurt cheese with honey and vanilla. Just before serving, spread yogurt mixture over meringue. Top with berries. Serve immediately.

Yogurt Cheese
Line a strainer with cheesecloth, paper towel or coffee filter. Place strainer over bowl. (You can also use a yogurt strainer, now readily available.) Place 3 cups (750 mL) unflavored yogurt in strainer. Cover and refrigerate for 3 hours or overnight. Discard liquid. Spoon thickened yogurt cheese into another container. Cover and refrigerate. Makes about 1 ½ cups (375 mL).

Chocolate Bread Pudding with Chocolate Bourbon Sauce

MAKES 8 SERVINGS

What a way to update an old-fashioned dessert! Orange, raspberry or coffee liqueur can be used in the sauce instead of Bourbon. You can also serve the sauce with angel cake (page 150), chocolate chunk squares (page 142), ice cream or fresh fruit.

Make Ahead
Sauce can be covered and refrigerated for up to a week. It will thicken when refrigerated, so soften slowly in a microwave or over hot water. Pudding can be covered and refrigerated overnight. Serve cold or reheat in a 225°F (105°C) oven for 15 minutes.

CHOCOLATE BREAD PUDDING

1/3 cup	butter	75 mL
6 oz	semisweet chocolate, chopped (about 1 1/2 cups/375 mL)	175 g
5	eggs	5
1/2 cup	granulated sugar	125 mL
1 1/2 cups	milk	375 mL
1 1/2 cups	light (5%) cream	375 mL
1 tsp	vanilla	5 mL
6 cups	egg bread or cinnamon bread cubes	1.5 L

CHOCOLATE BOURBON SAUCE

6 oz	semisweet chocolate, chopped (about 1 1/2 cups/375 mL)	175 g
1/4 cup	butter	50 mL
1/4 cup	corn syrup	50 mL
1/2 cup	whipping (35%) cream	125 mL
3 tbsp	Bourbon	45 mL

1. To prepare pudding, melt butter and chocolate in a stainless-steel bowl over simmering water. Stir together and cool slightly.

2. In a large bowl, whisk together eggs and sugar. Stir in milk, light cream, vanilla and melted chocolate. Stir in bread cubes. Let stand for 30 minutes.

3. Pour mixture into a buttered 8-inch (2 L) square baking dish. Place on a baking sheet in case of overflow. Convection bake in a preheated 325°F (160°C) oven for 35 to 40 minutes, or until a knife inserted in center comes out clean. Cool for at least 45 minutes before serving.

4. Meanwhile, to prepare sauce, combine chocolate, butter, corn syrup, whipping cream and Bourbon in a stainless-steel bowl. Place over hot water until chocolate melts. Whisk to blend ingredients together. Serve warm or at room temperature.

Pumpkin Praline Pie

MAKES ONE
9-INCH (23 CM) PIE

The praline surprise is tucked under the shiny surface of this classic pumpkin pie. Serve with or without whipped cream.

Make Ahead

The pastry, praline and filling can all be prepared ahead and refrigerated overnight (this is particularly helpful if you are making several pies at once). Before baking, simply pour the filling into the prepared pie shells and bake.

ALL-PURPOSE PASTRY

1 ½ cups	all-purpose flour	375 mL
1 tsp	salt	5 mL
¼ cup	cold butter, cut in cubes	50 mL
¼ cup	cold lard, cut in cubes	50 mL
1 tsp	lemon juice or white vinegar	5 mL
⅓ cup	ice-cold water (approx.)	75 mL

PRALINE

3 tbsp	butter	45 mL
½ cup	packed brown sugar	125 mL
½ cup	chopped pecans or hazelnuts	125 mL

FILLING

2	eggs	2
1	14-oz (398 mL) can pumpkin puree	1
¾ cup	packed brown sugar	175 mL
1 ¼ cups	evaporated milk	300 mL
1 tsp	ground cinnamon	5 mL
½ tsp	ground ginger	2 mL
¼ tsp	salt	1 mL
Pinch	ground cloves	Pinch
Pinch	ground nutmeg	Pinch

1. To make pastry, in a large bowl, combine flour and salt. Add butter and lard and cut in until mixture is in tiny bits. Combine lemon juice and water and sprinkle over flour. Mix together gently with a fork until mixture starts to come together. If it is too dry, add water 1 tsp (5 mL) at a time until mixture can be formed into a ball. (To make pastry in a food processor, combine flour and salt in bowl fitted with metal blade and pulse on/off. Add butter and lard and pulse until fat is in small bits. Combine lemon juice with ¼ cup (50 mL) cold water and pour over flour. Pulse just until dough starts to come together. Remove dough from food processor and form into ball.)

Rhubarb Coffee Cake (page 146)

2. On a lightly floured surface, roll pastry into a 12-inch (30 cm) circle. Line a 9-inch (23 cm) pie plate and double pastry over at rim to make a high fluted edge. Refrigerate.

3. To make praline, in a small saucepan, melt together butter and sugar over medium heat. Stir in pecans. Remove from heat and refrigerate until cool. Sprinkle praline over bottom of prepared pastry.

4. To prepare filling, in a large bowl, mix together eggs, pumpkin and sugar. Whisk in evaporated milk, cinnamon, ginger, salt, cloves and nutmeg. Pour mixture into pie shell.

5. Convection bake or roast in a preheated 400°F (200°C) oven for 10 minutes. Reduce heat to 325°F (160°C) and continue to bake for 45 to 50 minutes, or until a sharp knife inserted in center comes out clean. Cool completely on a rack.

Apple Pie with Cheddar Pastry (page 156)

Open-face Apricot Tart

MAKES ONE
10-INCH (25 CM) TART

This is a versatile recipe; instead of apricots you can use almost any seasonal fruit, such as plums, peaches, pears, rhubarb and apples (apricots and plums work well together).

If you do not have a rimless baking sheet, turn a rimmed baking sheet upside down to allow the tart to slide off easily.

PASTRY

2 cups	all-purpose flour	500 mL
2 tbsp	granulated sugar	25 mL
¼ tsp	salt	1 mL
¾ cup	cold butter, cut in pieces	175 mL
1	egg yolk	1
⅓ cup	ice-cold water	75 mL

FILLING

¼ cup	chopped pecans or almonds	50 mL
¼ cup	all-purpose flour	50 mL
⅓ cup	granulated sugar, divided	75 mL
1½ lbs	fresh apricots, pitted and quartered	750 g
1 tbsp	butter	15 mL
¼ cup	apricot jam	50 mL

1. To prepare pastry, combine flour, sugar and salt in a large bowl. Using a pastry blender or two knives, cut in butter until mixture resembles coarse crumbs with a few larger pieces. In a measuring cup, combine egg yolk and water. Pour over flour mixture, stirring with a fork. Bring mixture together to form a ball, adding more liquid if necessary. Shape into a disc. Wrap in plastic and refrigerate for 30 minutes.

2. Roll pastry out on a lightly floured surface to a 14-inch (35 cm) circle. Transfer pastry to a rimless baking sheet.

3. For the filling, in a small bowl, combine nuts, flour and ¼ cup (50 mL) sugar. Sprinkle over pastry to within 2 inches (5 cm) of edge.

4. Arrange apricots over nut mixture. Fold up border over fruit, crimping or folding pastry as necessary. Sprinkle fruit with remaining 2 tbsp (25 mL) sugar and dot with butter.

5. Convection bake or roast in a preheated 400°F (200°C) oven for 15 minutes. Reduce heat to 350°F (180°C) and continue to bake for 35 to 40 minutes, or until pastry is golden and fruit is tender. Carefully remove tart from oven. Cool for 4 minutes before gently sliding onto a rack.

6. Melt jam in a small saucepan over low heat. Spoon or brush melted jam over filling.

Convection Toaster Oven

Mediterranean Stuffed Mushrooms *164*

Baked Brie. *165*

Crab Melts. *166*

Tomato and Olive Bruschetta. *167*

Old-fashioned Macaroni and Cheese. *168*

Stuffed Baked Potatoes *169*

Rainbow Pepper Salad *170*

Baked Lemon Salmon with Mango Salsa. *171*

Halibut Provençal *172*

Roast Chicken with Orange and Sage *173*

Tandoori Chicken with Raita *174*

Peameal Bacon Roast *175*

Thai Pork Tenderloin *176*

Striploin Steak Roast with Green Sauce. *177*

Homestyle Meatloaf *178*

Raisin and Rosemary Soda Bread. *179*

Citrus Tea Bread. *180*

Baked Apples *181*

Blueberry Almond Crisp. *182*

Baked Rice Pudding *183*

Mediterranean Stuffed Mushrooms

MAKES 5
TO 6 SERVINGS

Serve these as a starter or as a side dish to accompany fish or poultry dishes. If jumbo mushrooms are unavailable, just use more of the smaller ones. To prevent mushrooms from wobbling, cut a small slice off the bottoms so they will sit flat. Six portobello mushrooms could also be substituted.

Make Ahead
Filling can be made ahead and refrigerated for up to six hours.

10 to 12	jumbo mushrooms (2½ to 3 inches/6 to 8 cm) in diameter	10 to 12
¾ cup	cooked brown or white rice	175 mL
2 tbsp	chopped oil-packed sun-dried tomatoes	25 mL
1	clove garlic, finely chopped	1
2	green onions, finely chopped	2
2 tbsp	chopped fresh dillweed	25 mL
2 tbsp	chopped fresh parsley	25 mL
½ cup	crumbled feta cheese (about 3 oz/90 g)	125 mL
½ tsp	salt	2 mL
¼ tsp	black pepper	1 mL
¼ cup	currants (optional)	50 mL
2 tbsp	olive oil	25 mL
2 tbsp	lemon juice	25 mL

1. Remove stems from mushrooms. Arrange in one layer on oven pan.

2. In a bowl, combine rice, sun-dried tomatoes, garlic, green onions, dill, parsley, feta, salt, pepper and currants, if using. Spoon into mushroom caps, mounding in center.

3. In a small measuring cup, combine olive oil and lemon juice. Drizzle over mushrooms.

4. Convection bake in a preheated 350°F (180°C) convection toaster oven for 12 to 15 minutes, or until mushrooms are cooked and filling is hot. Let stand for 2 minutes before serving.

Baked Brie

A creamy, oozing spread that can be served at almost any time — for brunch, afternoon tea, as an appetizer or dessert. Let your imagination be the guide for toppings — try hot pepper jelly, mango chutney, mango salsa (page 171), cranberry pear relish (page 47), green sauce (page 177) or your favorite jam or jelly. Serve with crackers, breads, raw vegetables or fruit. Line the oven pan with parchment paper for easy cleanup.

1	7-oz (200 g) round Brie cheese	1
⅓ cup	peach or apricot jam	75 mL
⅓ cup	cranberry sauce	75 mL
2 tbsp	toasted pine nuts	25 mL

1. Place Brie on parchment-lined oven pan (make sure paper does not hang over edges).
2. In a bowl, combine peach jam, cranberry sauce and pine nuts. Spoon over Brie.
3. Convection bake in a preheated 350°F (180°C) convection toaster oven for 8 to 10 minutes, or until cheese has softened.

Pecan and Brown Sugar Topping
In a small bowl, combine ½ cup (125 mL) packed brown sugar, ¼ cup (50 mL) chopped pecans and 1 tsp (5 mL) grated lemon zest. Spoon over Brie and continue with Step 3.

Fig and Port Topping
In a medium saucepan, combine 1 cup (250 mL) chopped dried figs with ½ cup (125 mL) orange juice and ½ cup (125 mL) Port. Bring to a boil and boil for 4 minutes. Turn off heat and let stand for 20 minutes. Spoon over Brie and continue with Step 3. Serve with fresh cracked walnuts.

Fresh Strawberry Salsa Topping
In a medium bowl, combine 1 cup (250 mL) coarsely chopped fresh strawberries, 1 chopped green onion, 2 tsp (10 mL) chopped jalapeño pepper, 1 tbsp (15 mL) olive oil and 1 tbsp (15 mL) orange juice. Bake Brie as in Step 3 and spoon salsa over before serving.

Crab Melts

This mixture also makes a great sandwich filling. As a substitute for crab, use diced imitation crab or even canned tuna.

1	7-oz (200 g) package frozen crab meat, defrosted	1
½ cup	diced Cheddar, Brie or Asiago cheese	125 mL
¼ cup	finely chopped celery	50 mL
¼ cup	finely chopped red bell pepper	50 mL
¼ cup	finely chopped green onion	50 mL
⅓ cup	mayonnaise	75 mL
1 tsp	Russian-style mustard	5 mL
½ tsp	salt	2 mL
¼ tsp	black pepper	1 mL
3	English muffins	3

1. Place crab in a sieve and press gently to squeeze out moisture. In a medium bowl, combine crab, cheese, celery, red pepper, green onion, mayonnaise, mustard, salt and pepper.

2. Cut English muffins in half horizontally. Place on oven pan. Convection bake in a preheated 350°F (180°C) convection toaster oven for 5 minutes.

3. Spread crab mixture evenly over muffins. Bake for 7 to 8 minutes, or until topping is heated through and cheese has melted slightly.

Tomato and Olive Bruschetta

MAKES 3
TO 6 SERVINGS

Serve this bruschetta
as a hearty starter.
The generous topping
is piled on top and
tumbles down the sides
of the bread, so provide
knives and forks.

¼ cup	olive oil, divided	50 mL
2	cloves garlic, minced	2
6	slices French or Italian bread, about 1 inch (2.5 cm) thick	6
3	tomatoes, cored and diced	3
½ cup	chopped green or black olives	125 mL
2 tbsp	balsamic vinegar	25 mL
¼ cup	shredded fresh basil	50 mL
¼ tsp	salt	1 mL
¼ tsp	black pepper	1 mL
6	thin slices Parmesan cheese (optional)	6

1. In a small bowl, combine 2 tbsp (25 mL) olive oil and garlic. Arrange bread slices on oven pan and brush with garlic oil.

2. Convection bake in a preheated 325°F (160°C) convection toaster oven for 8 to 10 minutes, or until slightly colored and toasty.

3. Meanwhile, in a medium bowl, combine tomatoes, olives, vinegar, remaining 2 tbsp (25 mL) oil, basil, salt and pepper.

4. Arrange toasts on serving plates. Spoon tomato mixture over bread. Top with Parmesan slices, if using.

Old-fashioned Macaroni and Cheese

MAKES 4
TO 6 SERVINGS

Convection baking in a shallow casserole gives this old-time favorite a golden, crispy crust.

1 ½ cups	uncooked macaroni (about 6 oz/175 g)	375 mL
2 tbsp	butter	25 mL
1	onion, chopped	1
2 tbsp	all-purpose flour	25 mL
2 cups	milk	500 mL
½ tsp	dry mustard	2 mL
¼ tsp	paprika	1 mL
¾ tsp	salt	4 mL
¼ tsp	black pepper	1 mL
1 ½ cups	grated Cheddar cheese	375 mL
1 cup	fresh bread crumbs	250 mL
2 tbsp	butter, melted	25 mL

1. In a large saucepan, cook macaroni in a large amount of boiling salted water for 8 to 10 minutes, or until just tender. Drain well.

2. Meanwhile, melt butter in a large saucepan over medium heat. Add onion and cook, stirring occasionally, for 3 to 4 minutes, or until softened. Add flour and cook, stirring, for 3 minutes.

3. Whisk in milk. Bring sauce to a boil, reduce heat and simmer, stirring occasionally, for 6 minutes. Remove from heat. Season with mustard, paprika, salt and pepper. Stir in cheese and drained macaroni. Spoon macaroni into a lightly greased 6-cup (1.5 L) shallow baking dish.

4. In a small bowl, stir together bread crumbs and melted butter. Sprinkle bread crumbs over macaroni.

5. Convection bake in a preheated 350°F (180°C) convection toaster oven for 25 minutes, or until golden and bubbling.

Stuffed Baked Potatoes

MAKES 4
TO 6 SERVINGS

Potatoes bake beautifully in the convection oven, especially when embellished with fresh herbs and cheese. Serve with cold meats, poultry or fish, or just with a salad for a light meal.

3	large baking potatoes	3
1/3 cup	sour cream or unflavored yogurt	75 mL
2 tbsp	olive oil or butter	25 mL
1 1/2 cups	grated Gruyère or Cheddar cheese, divided	375 mL
1/4 cup	chopped green onion or chives	50 mL
2 tsp	chopped fresh tarragon, or 1/2 tsp (2 mL) dried	10 mL
1/2 tsp	salt	2 mL
1/4 tsp	black pepper	1 mL
1/2 cup	diced cooked bacon or ham	125 mL

1. Pierce potatoes with a fork. Convection bake in a preheated 400°F (200°C) convection toaster oven, directly on rack, for 50 minutes, or until tender when pierced with a skewer. Cool slightly.

2. Carefully cut potatoes in half lengthwise. Gently scoop out potato pulp, leaving enough shell to act as a container. Place pulp in a large bowl and mash. Add sour cream, olive oil, 3/4 cup (175 mL) cheese, green onion, tarragon, salt, pepper and bacon. Mix well.

3. Spoon mixture into potato shells, mounding in center. Sprinkle with remaining 3/4 cup (175 mL) cheese.

4. Arrange potatoes on oven pan. Convection bake in a preheated 400°F (200°C) convection toaster oven for 12 to 15 minutes, or until potatoes are heated through and cheese has melted.

Rainbow Pepper Salad

MAKES 4
TO 5 SERVINGS

Make this versatile salad in late summer when multi-colored peppers are overflowing at the market. Serve it with egg dishes, polenta, pasta, fish and poultry. Cut the peppers into smaller pieces to use as a topping for grilled bread or as a sandwich filling.

Make Ahead
Salad can be served at room temperature or covered and refrigerated for up to two days.

3	bell peppers (red, yellow and orange), seeded and cut in 1-inch (2.5 cm) pieces	3
2 tbsp	olive oil	25 mL
1	onion, thinly sliced lengthwise	1
4	cloves garlic, peeled and cut in slivers	4
1/2 tsp	salt	2 mL
1/4 tsp	black pepper	1 mL
2 tbsp	balsamic vinegar	25 mL
2 tsp	capers	10 mL
2 tsp	chopped fresh oregano or basil, or 1/2 tsp (2 mL) dried	10 mL
Pinch	granulated sugar	Pinch
2	anchovy fillets, chopped (optional)	2

1. In a large bowl, combine peppers, olive oil, onion, garlic, salt and pepper. Toss.

2. Turn peppers into a lightly greased baking dish that will fit in oven. Convection bake in a preheated 400°F (200°C) convection toaster oven for 30 minutes, stirring twice during baking.

3. Remove peppers from oven and let cool for 15 minutes. Stir in vinegar, capers, oregano, sugar and anchovies, if using. Taste and adjust seasonings if necessary.

Baked Lemon Salmon with Mango Salsa

MAKES 4 SERVINGS

This is perfect for a quick weeknight meal. Papaya or pineapple could be used in place of mango.

Make Ahead

Prepare salsa, cover and refrigerate for up to six hours before serving. Cook salmon, cover and refrigerate up to a day ahead. Serve cold as part of a salad plate.

2 tbsp	lemon juice	25 mL
1 tbsp	olive oil	15 mL
1 tbsp	grated lemon zest	15 mL
2 tsp	Russian-style mustard	10 mL
1/2 tsp	black pepper	2 mL
4	salmon fillets (about 6 oz/175 g each), skin removed	4

MANGO SALSA

1	ripe mango, peeled and diced	1
2	green onions, finely chopped	2
1/4 cup	chopped red bell pepper	50 mL
2 tbsp	chopped fresh cilantro	25 mL
2 tbsp	lime juice	25 mL

1. In a small bowl, whisk together lemon juice, olive oil, lemon zest, mustard and pepper. Place salmon in an 8-inch (2 L) baking dish and pour marinade over fish. Marinate, refrigerated, for 20 minutes.

2. Arrange fillets on a lightly greased broiler rack placed over oven pan. Convection bake in a preheated 400°F (200°C) convection toaster oven for 10 to 12 minutes, or until salmon is just cooked in center.

3. Meanwhile, to prepare salsa, in a medium bowl, combine mango, green onions, red pepper, cilantro and lime juice. Serve with salmon.

Halibut Provençal

MAKES 4 SERVINGS

Fish retains both flavor and moistness when topped with this sauce and cooked quickly in a convection toaster oven. If halibut is unavailable, try cod, snapper or tilapia. Serve with rice or couscous.

SAUCE

2 tbsp	olive oil	25 mL
1	small onion, chopped	1
2	cloves garlic, finely chopped	2
½ cup	dry white wine	125 mL
1 cup	chopped tomato	250 mL
1 tsp	grated orange zest	5 mL
½ tsp	dried thyme leaves	2 mL
½ tsp	salt	2 mL
½ tsp	black pepper	2 mL

FISH

1 tbsp	olive oil	15 mL
1 tbsp	lemon juice	15 mL
¼ tsp	salt	1 mL
¼ tsp	black pepper	1 mL
1 ½ lbs	halibut fillets, cut in 4 pieces	750 g
⅓ cup	pitted black olives	75 mL
2 tsp	capers	10 mL
2 tbsp	chopped fresh basil or parsley	25 mL

1. To make sauce, in a medium skillet, heat oil over medium-high heat. Add onion and garlic. Cook, stirring occasionally, for 3 minutes. Add wine, tomato, orange zest, thyme, salt and pepper. Bring to a boil, reduce heat and simmer for 8 minutes.

2. Meanwhile, lightly grease broiler rack and place over oven pan (add ¼ cup/50 mL water to pan). To prepare fish, in a shallow dish, combine olive oil, lemon juice, salt and pepper. Dip fish into marinade, then place on broiler rack.

3. Place rack under preheated broiler in top position of convection toaster oven. Leave door ajar. Broil for 6 to 8 minutes per side, or until fish flakes lightly with a fork (timing depends on thickness of fish). Place fish on a serving platter. Spoon sauce over fish and top with olives, capers and basil.

Roast Chicken
with Orange and Sage

MAKES 4
TO 5 SERVINGS

A small chicken cooks to a beautiful golden brown in the convection toaster oven, and it is easy to prepare. Garnish with fresh orange sections and serve with a rice pilaf or mashed potatoes, or chill thoroughly and serve with potato salad.

1	3-lb (1.5 kg) chicken, patted dry	1
½ tsp	salt, divided	2 mL
½ tsp	black pepper, divided	2 mL
½	orange, cut in sections	½
4	cloves garlic, peeled and halved	4
3	sprigs fresh sage, or 1 tsp (5 mL) dried	3

1. Season inside of chicken with ¼ tsp (1 mL) salt and ¼ tsp (1 mL) pepper. Place orange sections, garlic and sage in cavity. Tuck chicken wing tips under back and tie legs together. Place breast side up on broiler rack set over oven pan. Sprinkle with remaining salt and pepper.

2. Convection bake in a preheated 350°F (180°C) convection toaster oven for 1 hour, or until juices run clear or a meat thermometer registers 180°F (82°C) when inserted into inner thigh.

3. Remove chicken from oven and cover with foil. Let stand for 15 minutes before carving.

Tandoori Chicken with Raita

MAKES 4 SERVINGS

This is a very relaxed version of chicken tandoori, which is traditionally cooked in a hot tandoor oven. The yogurt and spice marinade tenderizes and flavors the chicken. Raita is a cooling yogurt salad often served with spicy dishes. It can also be served as a spread or dip.

Make Ahead

Raita can be covered and refrigerated up to four hours before serving. Chicken is excellent cooked ahead and served chilled and sliced with a salad or on a buffet.

TANDOORI CHICKEN

½ cup	unflavored yogurt	125 mL
2	cloves garlic, minced	2
2 tsp	chopped gingerroot	10 mL
2 tbsp	lemon juice	25 mL
½ tsp	paprika	2 mL
½ tsp	ground cumin	2 mL
½ tsp	ground coriander	2 mL
¼ tsp	ground cardamom or cinnamon	1 mL
¼ tsp	cayenne pepper	1 mL
4	skinless, boneless chicken breasts (about 6oz/175g each)	4

RAITA

½	English cucumber, grated	½
½ tsp	salt	2 mL
¾ cup	unflavored yogurt	175 mL
½ cup	grated carrot	125 mL
½ tsp	granulated sugar	2 mL
¼ tsp	ground cumin	1 mL
2 tbsp	chopped fresh chives or green onion	25 mL
2 tbsp	chopped fresh mint	25 mL

1. To prepare chicken, in a small bowl, combine yogurt, garlic, ginger, lemon juice, paprika, cumin, coriander, cardamom and cayenne. Arrange chicken breasts in a single layer in an 8-inch (2 L) baking dish. Pour marinade over chicken and turn chicken to coat. Cover and refrigerate for 6 to 24 hours.

2. Arrange chicken breasts on lightly greased broiler rack set over oven pan. Convection bake in a preheated 350°F (180°C) convection toaster oven for 30 to 35 minutes, or until juices run clear.

3. Meanwhile, to prepare raita, combine grated cucumber with salt in a sieve placed over a bowl. Let stand for 25 minutes. Gently squeeze out excess moisture.

4. In a clean bowl, combine cucumber, yogurt, carrot, sugar, cumin, chives and mint. Taste and adjust seasonings if necessary. Serve with chicken.

Peameal Bacon Roast

MAKES 4
TO 6 SERVINGS

For a different type of roast, try peameal bacon. Serve with stir-fried rice or sweet potatoes and a tomato onion salad. Keep this recipe in your cottage or chalet file.

¼ cup	pineapple juice	50 mL
¼ cup	maple syrup	50 mL
1 tbsp	Dijon mustard	15 mL
1	peameal bacon roast (about 1 ½ lbs/750 g)	1
2 cups	fresh or canned pineapple chunks	500 mL

1. In a small bowl, whisk together pineapple juice, maple syrup and mustard.

2. Arrange roast in a shallow baking dish that will fit in oven.

3. Convection bake in a preheated 400°F (200°C) convection toaster oven for 35 minutes. Arrange pineapple chunks around roast and continue to bake for 30 to 35 minutes, or until a meat thermometer registers 160°F (70°C). Spoon glaze over bacon every 10 minutes during last half of cooking time. Let stand for 10 minutes before carving.

Stir-fried Rice

Heat 2 tbsp (25 mL) vegetable oil in a wok or large saucepan over medium-high heat. Add 1 thinly sliced onion, 2 thinly sliced stalks celery and 1 cup (250 mL) sliced mushrooms. Stir-fry for 4 minutes. Add 3 cups (750 mL) cold cooked rice and ½ cup (125 mL) fresh or frozen green peas. Stir-fry for 6 to 8 minutes, or until rice is heated through. Add 2 beaten eggs. Continue to stir-fry for 4 minutes, or until eggs are cooked. Stir in 2 tbsp (25 mL) soy sauce and 2 chopped green onions. Makes 5 to 6 servings.

Thai Pork Tenderloin

MAKES 5
TO 6 SERVINGS

An easy preparation for a tender full-flavored pork tenderloin. Serve hot with steamed broccoli and stir-fried rice (page 175) or chill and slice thinly for sandwiches, salads or meat trays. For a less spicy version, reduce the sweet Asian chili sauce to 1 tbsp (15 mL).

2	cloves garlic, minced	2
1 tbsp	chopped gingerroot	15 mL
2 tbsp	chopped fresh cilantro	25 mL
3 tbsp	hoisin sauce	45 mL
2 tbsp	lime juice or lemon juice	25 mL
1 tbsp	fish sauce or soy sauce	15 mL
1 tbsp	sesame oil	15 mL
2 tbsp	sweet Asian chili sauce	25 mL
2	pork tenderloins (about 12 oz/375 g each)	2

1. In a small bowl, combine garlic, ginger, cilantro, hoisin, lime juice, fish sauce, sesame oil and chili sauce.

2. Arrange tenderloins in a single layer in a dish just large enough to hold pork. Pour sauce over meat, turning tenderloins to coat. Cover and refrigerate for 1 to 24 hours.

3. Arrange tenderloin with sauce on parchment paper cut to fit oven pan.

4. Convection bake in a preheated 350°F (180°C) convection toaster oven for 25 to 30 minutes, or until juices run clear when tenderloin is pierced. Let stand for 5 minutes, then slice on the diagonal.

Fish Sauce
Fish sauce is a thin, brown, salty liquid made from fermented or pickled fish. It is sold in large bottles and is used instead of salt in Thai cooking. If it is unavailable, use soy sauce.

Striploin Steak Roast with Green Sauce

MAKES 3
TO 4 SERVINGS

A thick striploin steak produces a small tender roast with the simplest of seasonings. Montreal steak spice is the secret ingredient. It is usually located in the spice/herb section of the supermarket, but you can also use your favorite seasoning mix. Green sauce (also called salsa verde) is a full-flavored condiment to serve alongside the carved steak. Just add sliced tomatoes, mashed potatoes or a pasta salad.

Make Ahead
Green sauce can be covered and refrigerated up to a day ahead.

GREEN SAUCE

½ cup	fresh parsley leaves	125 mL
3	green onions, coarsely chopped	3
1	slice white bread, crust removed, cubed	1
1 tbsp	red wine vinegar	15 mL
1	anchovy fillet, mashed, or 1 tsp (5 mL) anchovy paste	1
2 tsp	capers	10 mL
¼ cup	olive oil	50 mL
¼ tsp	salt	1 mL
¼ tsp	black pepper	1 mL

ROAST

2	cloves garlic, minced	2
1 tbsp	lime juice or lemon juice	15 mL
1 tbsp	Worcestershire sauce	15 mL
1 tbsp	olive oil	15 mL
1 tbsp	Montreal steak spice	15 mL
1	striploin steak (about 1 lb/500 g), 1½ inches (4 cm) thick	1

1. To prepare sauce, chop parsley and green onions in food processor. Add bread cubes, vinegar, anchovy and capers. Puree, then pour in olive oil and combine well. Season with salt and pepper.

2. For the roast, combine garlic, lime juice, Worcestershire sauce and olive oil in a flat dish. Trim fat from steak. Dip both sides of steak into mixture, then roll steak in spice to coat. Place on broiler rack set over bake pan.

3. Convection bake in a preheated 375°F (190°C) convection toaster oven for 22 to 25 minutes, or until a meat thermometer registers 140°F (60°C) for rare to medium-rare. Cover with foil. Let stand for 10 minutes before carving in thin slices. Serve with green sauce.

Homestyle Meatloaf

MAKES 6 SERVINGS

This old standby is still a big favorite. Instead of ground beef you can use a combination of ground meats such as pork, veal, turkey or chicken. Serve leftovers in sandwiches.

1 tbsp	olive oil	15 mL
1	onion, chopped	1
3	cloves garlic, finely chopped	3
1½ lbs	lean ground beef	750 g
1	egg	1
½ cup	dry bread crumbs	125 mL
½ cup	ketchup or chili sauce	125 mL
1 tbsp	horseradish	15 mL
1 tbsp	Worcestershire sauce	15 mL
1 tbsp	Dijon mustard	15 mL
½ tsp	dried sage leaves	2 mL
½ tsp	salt	2 mL
¼ tsp	black pepper	1 mL

TOPPING

¼ cup	ketchup	50 mL
1 tsp	horseradish	5 mL
1 tsp	Dijon mustard	5 mL

1. In a small skillet, heat oil over medium-high heat. Add onion and garlic. Cook, stirring occasionally, for 3 minutes, or until softened.

2. In a large bowl, combine ground beef, egg, bread crumbs, ketchup, horseradish, Worcestershire, mustard, sage, salt, pepper and cooked onion mixture. Mix together thoroughly. Pack into an 8- by 4-inch (1.5 L) loaf pan.

3. For topping, in small bowl, combine ketchup, horseradish and mustard. Spread over meatloaf. Convection bake in a preheated 350°F (180°C) convection toaster oven for 60 to 70 minutes, or until a meat thermometer registers 170°F (77°C). Let stand for 5 minutes. Pour off any accumulated fat before serving.

Raisin and Rosemary Soda Bread

MAKES ONE
9-INCH (23 CM) LOAF

Ireland's most popular bread bakes perfectly in the convection oven. For more even browning, turn the bread at half time. For a plain loaf, omit the rosemary and raisins.

2 ½ cups	all-purpose flour	625 mL
½ cup	whole wheat flour	125 mL
1 tsp	salt	5 mL
1 tsp	baking soda	5 mL
1 tbsp	chopped fresh rosemary, or 1 ½ tsp (7 mL) dried	15 mL
1 cup	golden raisins	250 mL
1 ¾ cups	buttermilk or unflavored yogurt	425 mL

1. In a large bowl, combine all-purpose flour, whole wheat flour, salt, baking soda, rosemary and raisins. Combine thoroughly.

2. Add buttermilk. Stir to combine but do not overmix (dough will be slightly sticky). Turn onto a floured surface. With floured hands, shape dough into a loaf about 9 inches (23 cm) long. Cut 5 diagonal slashes in top. Place on lightly floured oven pan.

3. Convection bake in a preheated 400°F (200°C) convection toaster oven for 20 minutes. Reduce heat to 350°F (180°C). Continue baking for 25 minutes, or until bread sounds hollow when tapped on bottom. Cool on rack.

Variations

Cheddar and Sun-dried Tomato Soda Bread: Omit rosemary and raisins. Add 1 cup (250 mL) grated Cheddar cheese and 3 tbsp (45 mL) chopped dry or oil-packed sun-dried tomatoes.

Apricot Caraway Soda Bread: Omit rosemary and raisins. Add ¾ cup (175 mL) diced dried apricots and 2 tsp (10 mL) caraway seeds.

Citrus Tea Bread

MAKES ONE 8- BY
4-INCH (1.5 L) LOAF

Simple and fresh
tasting, this tea
bread can be served plain
or with fresh or stewed
fruit. The bread freezes
well, so serve half now,
wrap the remaining and
freeze for up to six weeks.

½ cup	butter, softened	125 mL
¾ cup	granulated sugar	175 mL
2	eggs	2
1 tbsp	grated lemon zest	15 mL
1 tbsp	grated orange zest	15 mL
1½ cups	all-purpose flour	375 mL
1 tsp	baking powder	5 mL
¼ tsp	salt	1 mL
½ cup	milk	125 mL
⅓ cup	confectioner's (icing) sugar	75 mL
3 tbsp	lemon juice	45 mL
3 tbsp	orange juice	45 mL

1. In a large bowl, cream butter and sugar until light. Beat in eggs one at a time. Stir in lemon and orange zest.

2. In a separate bowl, combine flour, baking powder and salt. Add alternately to butter mixture with milk, making three liquid and two dry additions. Spoon into a greased and parchment-lined 8- by 4-inch (1.5 L) loaf pan.

3. Convection bake in a preheated 350°F (180°C) convection toaster oven for 45 minutes, or until a cake tester inserted in center comes out clean (rotate bread halfway through baking time).

4. Meanwhile, in a measuring cup, combine icing sugar, lemon juice and orange juice. Stir to dissolve sugar. Using a skewer, pierce baked loaf in several places. Gradually spoon glaze over loaf. Cool loaf for 15 minutes before removing from pan. Cool completely on a rack.

Variation
Citrus Herb Bread: Add 2 tsp (10 mL) chopped fresh thyme, rosemary, lemon verbena or lavender flowers to batter with grated citrus zest.

Baked Apples

MAKES 4 SERVINGS

Sometimes a forgotten dessert, baked apples are an appealing addition to any dessert table. If the apples are browning too much, reduce the oven temperature to 325°F (160°C) toward the end of the baking time. Serve warm with ice cream or flavored yogurt cheese (page 182).

4	apples (such as Northern Spy, Ida Red, Golden Delicious)	4
¼ cup	maple syrup	50 mL
¼ cup	apricot jam	50 mL
¼ cup	apple juice or water	50 mL
2 tbsp	lemon juice	25 mL
¼ tsp	ground nutmeg	1 mL

1. Core apples using apple corer or melon ball scoop. Using a sharp knife, score peel about a third of the way down apples (this prevents apples from bursting). Arrange apples in a shallow baking pan that will hold juices.

2. In a small bowl, combine syrup, jam, apple juice, lemon juice and nutmeg. Spoon into center of apples, letting remainder drizzle over.

3. Convection bake in a preheated 375°F (190°C) convection toaster oven for 25 minutes. Spoon some glaze over apples. Rotate pan. Bake for another 20 to 25 minutes, or until apples are tender.

Meatless Dinner for 4

Prepare the soup ahead of time and heat just before serving. Bake the quesadillas after guests arrive, or bake ahead and serve at room temperature as hors d'oeuvres or as an accompaniment to the soup. Cook the curry while serving the appetizer and soup. Make the apples ahead and reheat at 300°F (150° C) for 10 minutes or serve at room temperature.

- Black Bean and Cheese Quesadillas (page 28)
- Squash and Parsnip Soup (page 31)
- Chickpea and Vegetable Curry (page 94)
- Steamed Brown Rice
- Green Salad
- Baked Apples (page 181)

Blueberry Almond Crisp

MAKES 6 SERVINGS

Instead of using only blueberries, you can try a combination of fruits such as blueberries and peaches, blueberries and raspberries or raspberries and peaches. If you are using juicy fruits like peaches, stir in an additional 1 tbsp (15 mL) flour.

Serve with Orange Yogurt Cheese.

4 cups	fresh or frozen blueberries	1 L
1 tbsp	all-purpose flour	15 mL
2 tsp	lemon juice	10 mL
½ tsp	almond extract	2 mL
TOPPING		
1 cup	rolled oats (not instant)	250 mL
½ cup	packed brown sugar	125 mL
¼ cup	all-purpose flour	50 mL
¼ cup	sliced or slivered almonds	50 mL
¼ cup	butter, melted	50 mL

1. Arrange blueberries in a lightly greased 8-inch (2 L) square baking dish. Sprinkle berries with flour, lemon juice and almond extract. Stir to distribute flour.

2. In a bowl, combine rolled oats, sugar, flour and almonds. Stir in butter. Spread topping over fruit.

3. Convection bake in a preheated 350°F (180°C) convection toaster oven for 25 minutes, or until top is golden and blueberries are bubbling.

Orange Yogurt Cheese
Place 1 cup (250 mL) unflavored yogurt in a sieve lined with cheesecloth, coffee filter or paper towel and place sieve over a bowl (or use a yogurt strainer). Cover and refrigerate for 3 to 4 hours. Place drained yogurt in a bowl. Stir in 2 tbsp (25 mL) orange juice, 1 tsp (5 mL) grated orange zest and 1 tbsp (15 mL) granulated sugar. Cover and refrigerate until using. Makes about ½ cup (125 mL).

Baked Rice Pudding

A perfect way to use extra cooked rice, this pudding is satisfying without being too rich. If you have a sweet tooth, add up to 2 tbsp (25 mL) sugar. I like to serve this cold, cut in squares or triangles and accompanied by fresh fruit.

Make Ahead
Pudding can be prepared, covered and refrigerated for up to a day before serving.

2	eggs	2
2 cups	milk	500 mL
¼ cup	packed brown sugar	50 mL
1 cup	cooked rice	250 mL
⅓ cup	dried blueberries, cranberries or golden raisins	75 mL
1 tsp	grated lemon or orange zest	5 mL
½ tsp	salt	2 mL
Pinch	ground nutmeg	Pinch

1. In a large bowl, beat eggs lightly. Add milk, sugar, rice, blueberries, lemon zest and salt. Combine thoroughly. Pour into a lightly greased 6-cup (1.5 L) shallow baking dish. Sprinkle with nutmeg.

2. Convection bake in a preheated 325°F (160°C) convection toaster oven for 35 to 40 minutes, or until a sharp knife inserted in center comes out clean. Let sit for 30 minutes before serving.

National Library of Canada Cataloguing in Publication

Stephen, Linda
The best convection oven cookbook / Linda Stephen.

Includes index.
ISBN 0-7788-0067-9

1. Convection oven cookery.
I. Title.

TX840.C65S84 2003   641.5'8   C2002-905889-9

Index

Adapting recipes. *See* Convection
cooking, converting
recipes.
Airplane Snacks, 20
Almonds
Almond Angel Cake, 150
Blueberry Almond Crisp, 182
Chocolate Almond Torte, 155
Aluminum foil. *See* Convection
cooking, use of foil in.
Angel cakes. *See* Cakes.
Appetizers. *See also* Salads, Soups.
Airplane Snacks, 20
Apricot Prosciutto Wraps, 22
Asian-flavored Meatballs, 70
Baked Brie, 165
Baked Cod with Pistou, 41
Black Bean and Cheese
Quesadillas, 28
Camembert Pesto Phyllo
Cups, 25
Cheddar Cheese Sticks, 157
Chicken Satay Quesadillas, 26
Crab Melts, 166
Eggplant Olive Tapenade, 27
Fish Cakes, 43
Fish Fillets with Miso
Dressing, 42
French Onion Soup
Bruschetta, 23
Ham and Cheese Quesadillas,
28
Honey Garlic Chicken Wings,
49
Mediterranean Stuffed
Mushrooms, 164
Salsa Nachos, 29
Savory Shortbread Bites, 21
Shrimp with Tomato and Feta,
44
Southwestern Wings, 30
Stuffed Baked Tomatoes, 101
Tomato and Olive Bruschetta,
167
Tomato Basil Pizzettes, 24
Apples
Apple Bran Muffins, 133

Apple Butter, 137
Apple Coffee Cake, 146
Apple Cranberry Strudel, 154
Apple Pie with Cheddar
Pastry, 156
Baked Apples, 181
Cabbage and Apple Salad, 91
Oven French Toast with
Caramelized Apples, 115
Roast Pork Loin with Apples,
72
Turnip and Apple Mash, 100
Apricots
Apricot Caraway Soda Bread,
179
Apricot Prosciutto Wraps, 22
Baked Ham with Apricot
Glaze, 71
Dried Cranberry and Apricot
Dressing, 58
Oatmeal Apricot Scones, 130
Open-face Apricot Tart, 162
Asian-flavored Meatballs, 70
Asparagus
Asparagus, Chèvre and
Smoked Salmon Frittata,
118
Roasted Asparagus, 77
Avocados, 32
Guacamole, 29

Bacon
Baked Spaghetti Carbonara,
85
Mushroom and Bacon Open-
face Sandwich, 121
Oven Home Fries with
Peameal Bacon, 120
Peameal Bacon Roast, 175
Baked Apples, 181
Baked Beets, 73
Baked Brie, 165
Baked Cod with Pistou, 41
Baked Ham with Apricot Glaze,
71
Baked Lemon Salmon with
Mango Salsa, 171

Baked potatoes. *See* Potatoes.
Baked Rice Pudding, 183
Baked Spaghetti Carbonara, 85
Baked Sweet Potatoes, 75
Baking paper. *See* Parchment
paper.
Bananas
Cranberry Banana Muffins,
132
Barbecue Sauce, 76
Bars. *See* Squares.
Basil. *See also* Pesto.
Tomato Basil Pizzettes, 24
Beans. *See also* Chipotles, Green
beans.
Black Bean and Cheese
Quesadillas, 28
Speedy Baked Beans, 87
Thyme-scented Leg of Lamb
with Beans, 78
Beef
Asian-flavored Meatballs, 70
Cheeseburger Pie, 66
Danish Meat Patties, 67
Deep-Dish Tamale Pie, 68
Herbed Flank Steak with
Polenta, 64
Homestyle Meatloaf, 178
Rib Eye Roast with Beer
Mushroom Gravy, 63
Roast Prime Rib of Beef, 62
safe temperatures for
doneness, 13
Striploin Steak Roast with
Green Sauce, 177
Beer Mushroom Gravy, 63
Beets
Baked Beets, 73
Berries. *See* Blueberries,
Cranberries, Raspberries,
Strawberries.
Biscuits
Blueberry Lemon Drop
Biscuits, 129
Chive Gruyère Biscuits, 128
Drop Cheddar Cornmeal
Biscuits, 69

Raspberry Lemon Drop
  Biscuits, 129
Rosemary Cheddar Biscuits,
  128
Black Bean and Cheese
  Quesadillas, 28
Bleach solution, 16
Blue cheese
  Roasted Pear Salad with
    Candied Pecans and Blue
    Cheese, 110
Blueberries
  Blueberry Almond Crisp, 182
  Blueberry Cinnamon Loaf,
    134
  Blueberry Coffee Cake, 146
  Blueberry Lemon Drop
    Biscuits, 129
  Quick Berry Jam, 137
Bonnie Stern's Pavlova, 158
Bran
  Apple Bran Muffins, 133
Bread crumbs, 39
Bread pudding. *See* Desserts.
Breaded Veal in Tomato Sauce,
  80
Breads. *See also* Bread crumbs,
    Croutons, Muffins,
    Quickbreads.
  Fontina and Grape Flatbread,
    109
  Monster Potato Hamburger
    Buns, 136
  Potato Bread, 137
  Roasted Garlic Bread, 140
  Rosemary Garlic Fougasse,
    138
  Whole Wheat Grain Bread,
    135
Breakfasts. *See* Brunch dishes.
Brie
  Baked Brie, 165
  Brie and Strawberry Crêpes,
    116
Broccoli Cheddar Gratin, 96
Broiled Cilantro Garlic Chicken
  Breasts, 53
Brunch dishes. *See also*
    Appetizers, Breads, Coffee
    cakes, Muffins,
    Quickbreads.
  Asparagus, Chèvre and
    Smoked Salmon Frittata,
    118
  Brie and Strawberry Crêpes,
    116
  Easy Cheese Soufflé, 122

Homemade Pizza, 124
Mushroom and Bacon
  Open-face Sandwich, 121
Oven French Toast with
  Caramelized Apples, 115
Oven Home Fries with
  Peameal Bacon, 120
Prosciutto Onion Quiche,
  119
Rise and Shine Granola, 114
Tofu with Sesame Hoisin
  Glaze, 123
Vegetable Strudel, 126
Bruschetta
  French Onion Soup
    Bruschetta, 23
  Tomato and Olive Bruschetta,
    167
Buns. *See* Breads.
Burgers
  Danish Meat Patties, 67
  Fish Cakes, 43
  Turkey Burgers with Corn
    Salsa, 60
Butters
  Apple Butter, 137

Cabbage
  Cabbage and Apple Salad, 91
  Cabbage Roll Bake, 82
  Colcannon Bake, 97
Cakes. *See also* Tortes.
  Almond Angel Cake, 150
  Apple Coffee Cake, 146
  Blueberry Coffee Cake, 146
  Carrot Cake, 148
  Ginger Gingerbread, 147
  Mocha Chocolate Chip Angel
    Cake, 150
  Peach Upside-down Cake, 149
  Rhubarb Coffee Cake, 146
Camembert Pesto Phyllo Cups,
  25
Caramelized apples, 115
Caramelized onions, 23
Caraway
  Apricot Caraway Soda Bread,
    179
Carrot Cake, 148
Casseroles. *See* One-Dish
    Suppers.
Cauliflower
  Roasted Cauliflower, 94
Cereals
  Rise and Shine Granola, 114
  Whole Wheat Grain Bread,
    135

Cheddar
  Apple Pie with Cheddar
    Pastry, 156
  Broccoli Cheddar Gratin, 96
  Cheddar and Sun-dried
    Tomato Soda Bread, 179
  Cheddar Cheese Sticks, 157
  Cheddar Sage Muffins, 131
  Drop Cheddar Cornmeal
    Biscuits, 69
  Easy Cheese Soufflé, 122
  Old-fashioned Macaroni and
    Cheese, 168
  Rosemary Cheddar Biscuits,
    128
  Spinach, Cheddar and Ham
    Frittata, 118
Cheese
  Apple Pie with Cheddar
    Pastry, 156
  Asparagus, Chèvre and
    Smoked Salmon Frittata,
    118
  Baked Brie, 165
  Black Bean and Cheese
    Quesadillas, 28
  Brie and Strawberry Crêpes,
    116
  Broccoli Cheddar Gratin, 96
  Camembert Pesto Phyllo
    Cups, 25
  Cheddar and Sun-dried
    Tomato Soda Bread, 179
  Cheddar Cheese Sticks, 157
  Cheddar Sage Muffins, 131
  Chive Gruyère Biscuits, 128
  Crab Melts, 166
  Drop Cheddar Cornmeal
    Biscuits, 69
  Easy Cheese Soufflé, 122
  Eggplant with Mozzarella and
    Tomato Sauce, 88
  Ham and Cheese Quesadillas,
    28
  Old-fashioned Macaroni and
    Cheese, 168
  Prosciutto Onion Quiche, 119
  Ricotta Orange Crêpes, 117
  Roasted Pear Salad with
    Candied Pecans and Blue
    Cheese, 110
  Rosemary Cheddar Biscuits,
    128
  Shrimp with Tomato and Feta,
    44
  Spinach, Cheddar and Ham
    Frittata, 118

Warm Chèvre Salad with
Mexican Pesto, 106
Cheeseburger Pie, 66
Chèvre. *See also* Goat cheese.
Asparagus, Chèvre and
Smoked Salmon Frittata,
118
Homemade Pizza, 124
Warm Chèvre Salad with
Mexican Pesto, 106
Chicken
Broiled Cilantro Garlic
Chicken Breasts, 53
Chicken and Spinach Pie, 92
Chicken Pot Pie, 56
Chicken Satay Quesadillas, 26
Chicken Souvlaki with
Tzatziki, 52
Chicken with Sesame Hoisin
Glaze, 123
Crispy Chicken with
Cranberry Pear Relish, 47
Honey Garlic Chicken Wings,
49
Roast Chicken with Orange
and Sage, 173
Roasted Drumsticks with
Vegetables, 48
Roasted Flat Chicken, 46
safe temperatures for
doneness, 13
Santa Fe Chicken Wraps, 86
Southwestern Wings, 30
Stuffed Chicken Breasts with
Goat Cheese and Red
Pepper Sauce, 50
stuffing, 13
Tandoori Chicken with Raita,
174
Chickpea and Vegetable Curry,
94
Chipotle peppers, 64
Chive Gruyère Biscuits, 128
Cider-glazed Turkey Breast, 57
Cilantro, 65
Broiled Cilantro Garlic
Chicken Breasts, 53
Warm Chèvre Salad with
Mexican Pesto, 106
Cinnamon
Blueberry Cinnamon Loaf,
134
Chocolate
Chocolate Almond Torte, 155
Chocolate Bread Pudding
with Chocolate Bourbon
Sauce, 159

Chocolate Chunk Cookie
Squares, 144
Lemon and White Chocolate
Napoleons, 152
Mocha Chocolate Chip Angel
Cake, 150
Citrus Herb Bread, 180
Citrus Tea Bread, 180
Classic Shortbread, 141
Cod
Baked Cod with Pistou, 41
Coffee cakes. *See* Cakes.
Colcannon Bake, 97
Condiments. *See also* Sauces.
Apple Butter, 137
Baked Brie toppings, 165
Caramelized onions, 23
Corn Salsa, 60
Cranberry Pear Relish, 47
Eggplant Olive Tapenade, 27
Fresh Tomato Salsa, 86
Green Sauce, 177
Mango Salsa, 171
Mexican Pesto, 106
Orange Yogurt Cheese, 182
Quick Berry Jam, 137
Yogurt Cheese, 158
Convection cooking, 11-18
about the recipes, 17
calibrating oven temperature,
17
convection bake, 12
convection broil, 14
convection roast, 13-14
converting and adapting
recipes, 14-15, 17
cookware and containers, 15-
16
covered foods, 14-15
general tips, 16
oven settings, 12-14
preheating, 14
racks, 12, 14
safety, 16-17
standing time, 14, 17
use of foil in, 16
use of parchment paper in, 15
Convection ovens. *See*
Convection cooking.
Convection toaster ovens, 17-18
Convection toaster oven recipes
Baked Apples, 181
Baked Brie, 165
Baked Lemon Salmon with
Mango Salsa, 171
Baked Rice Pudding, 183
Blueberry Almond Crisp, 182

Citrus Tea Bread, 180
Crab Melts, 166
converting recipes, 17
Halibut Provençal, 172
Homestyle Meatloaf, 178
Mediterranean Stuffed
Mushrooms, 164
Old-fashioned Macaroni and
Cheese, 168
Peameal Bacon Roast, 175
Rainbow Pepper Salad, 170
Raisin and Rosemary Soda
Bread, 179
Roast Chicken with Orange
and Sage, 173
Striploin Steak Roast with
Green Sauce, 177
Stuffed Baked Potatoes, 169
Tandoori Chicken with Raita,
174
Thai Pork Tenderloin, 176
Tomato and Olive Bruschetta,
167
Conventional oven. *See*
Convection cooking,
converting and adapting
recipes.
Converting recipes. *See*
Convection cooking,
converting and adapting
recipes.
Cookies
Chocolate Chunk Cookie
Squares, 144
Classic Shortbread, 141
Date Squares, 143
Lavender Shortbread, 141
Lemon Rosemary Shortbread,
141
Oatmeal Crisp Cookies, 142
Savory Shortbread Bites, 21
Coriander. *See* Cilantro.
Corn Salsa, 60
Cornish Hens with Wild Rice
and Mushrooms, 54
Cornmeal. *See* Polenta.
Couscous
Stuffed Baked Tomatoes, 101
Crab Melts, 166
Cranberries
Apple Cranberry Strudel, 154
Cranberry Banana Muffins,
132
Cranberry Pear Relish, 47
Dried Cranberry and Apricot
Dressing, 58
Creole Sauce, 74

Crêpes
  Brie and Strawberry Crêpes, 116
  Mushroom, Spinach and Ham Crêpes, 117
  Ricotta Orange Crêpes, 117
Crisps. See Desserts.
Crispy Butterflied Pork Chops with Creole Sauce, 74
Crispy Chicken with Cranberry Pear Relish, 47
Croutons, 104
Crouton Cups, 112
Cucumbers
  Cucumber Salad, 35
  Raita, 174
  Tzatziki, 52
Currants
  Oatmeal Currant Scones, 130
Curries
  Chickpea and Vegetable Curry, 94

Danish Meat Patties, 67
Date Squares, 143
Deep-Dish Tamale Pie, 68
Desserts. See also Cookies.
  Almond Angel Cake, 150
  Apple Cranberry Strudel, 154
  Apple Pie with Cheddar Pastry, 156
  Baked Apples, 181
  Baked Rice Pudding, 183
  Blueberry Almond Crisp, 182
  Bonnie Stern's Pavlova, 158
  Carrot Cake, 148
  Chocolate Almond Torte, 155
  Chocolate Bread Pudding with Chocolate Bourbon Sauce, 159
  Ginger Gingerbread, 147
  Lemon and White Chocolate Napoleons, 152
  Open-face Apricot Tart, 162
  Peach Upside-down Cake, 149
  Pumpkin Praline Pie, 160
  Rhubarb Coffee Cake, 146
  Strawberry Rhubarb Crunch, 151
Dips. See also Spreads.
  Guacamole, 29
  Raita, 174
  Savory Dip, 30
  Tzatziki, 52
Dressings. See Stuffings.
Dried Cranberry and Apricot Dressing, 58

Drop Cheddar Cornmeal Biscuits, 69

Edible flowers, 154
Eggplant
  Eggplant Olive Tapenade, 27
  Eggplant with Mozzarella and Tomato Sauce, 88
  Mediterranean Vegetables with Orzo, 103
  Roasted Eggplant Salad, 88
Eggs. See also Meringues.
  Asparagus, Chèvre and Smoked Salmon Frittata, 118
  Easy Cheese Soufflé, 122
  Oven French Toast with Caramelized Apples, 115
  Prosciutto Onion Quiche, 119
  Spinach, Cheddar and Ham Frittata, 118

Fennel
  Olives with Fennel and Orange, 93
  Roasted Portobello Mushroom and Fennel Salad, 108
Feta
  Shrimp with Tomato and Feta, 44
First courses. See Appetizers.
Fish. See also Seafood.
  Asparagus, Chèvre and Smoked Salmon Frittata, 118
  Baked Cod with Pistou, 41
  Baked Lemon Salmon with Mango Salsa, 171
  Fish Cakes, 43
  Fish Fillets with Miso Dressing, 42
  Fish sauce, 176
  Halibut Provençal, 172
  Hoisin Orange Salmon, 35
  Lemon and Dill Fish Kabobs, 37
  Maple Glazed Salmon, 34
  Mom's Salmon Loaf, 36
  Red Snapper with Herbed Bread Crumbs and Tartar Sauce, 38
  Tilapia Mexicana, 40
Flank steak. See Beef
Flatbread. See Breads.
Flowers. See Edible flowers.
Foil. See Convection cooking, use of foil in.

Fontina and Grape Flatbread, 109
Food safety. See Safety.
French Onion Soup Bruschetta, 23
French toast
  Oven French Toast with Caramelized Apples, 115
Fresh Tomato Salsa, 86
Frikadeller. See Danish Meat Patties.
Frittatas
  Asparagus, Chèvre and Smoked Salmon Frittata, 118
  Spinach, Cheddar and Ham Frittata, 118
Fruit. See individual fruits.

Garlic
  Broiled Cilantro Garlic Chicken Breasts, 53
  roasted, 32, 140
  Roasted Garlic Bread, 140
  Roasted Tomato and Garlic Soup, 32
  Rosemary Garlic Fougasse, 138
Ginger Gingerbread, 147
Gingerbread. See Cakes.
Glazed Spareribs, 76
Goat cheese. See also Chèvre, Feta.
  Stuffed Chicken Breasts with Goat Cheese and Red Pepper Sauce, 50
Granola
  Rise and Shine Granola, 114
Grapes
  Fontina and Grape Flatbread, 109
Gratins. See also Casseroles.
  Broccoli Cheddar Gratin, 96
Gravies
  Beer Mushroom Gravy, 63
Greek Salad in Kaiser Crouton Cups, 112
Green beans
  Potato and Bean Caesar Salad, 105
Ground beef. See Beef.
Gruyère
  Chive Gruyère Biscuits, 128
Guacamole, 29

Halibut Provençal, 172
Ham. See also Bacon, Prosciutto.
  Baked Ham with Apricot Glaze, 71

Ham and Cheese Quesadillas, 28

Mushroom, Spinach and Ham Crêpes, 117

safe temperature for doneness, 13

Spinach, Cheddar and Ham Frittata, 118

Hamburger buns. *See* Breads.

Herbed Flank Steak with Polenta, 64

Herbes de Provence, 23

Hoisin sauce

Chicken with Sesame Hoisin Glaze, 123

Hoisin Orange Salmon, 35

Tofu with Sesame Hoisin Glaze, 123

Home fries, 120

Homemade Pizza, 124

Homestyle Meatloaf, 178

Honey Garlic Chicken Wings, 49

Hors d'oeuvres. *See* Appetizers.

Jams

Quick Berry Jam, 137

Kabobs. *See also* Satays.

Lemon and Dill Fish Kabobs, 37

Kaiser Crouton Cups, 112

Lamb

Roasted Rack of Lamb, 77

safe temperature for doneness, 13

Thyme-scented leg of Lamb with Beans, 78

Lavender Shortbread, 141

Lemons

Baked Lemon Salmon with Mango Salsa, 171

Lemon and Dill Fish Kabobs, 37

Lemon and White Chocolate Mousse, 152

Lemon and White Chocolate Napoleons, 152

Lemon Rosemary Shortbread, 141

Loaves. *See* Breads, Quickbreads.

Lunches. *See* Appetizers, Brunch dishes.

Macaroni. *See* Pastas.

Mango Salsa, 171

Maple-glazed Salmon, 34

Meat. *See* Beef, Ham, Lamb, Pork, Veal.

Meatballs. *See also* Burgers.

Asian-flavored Meatballs, 70

Meatless main courses. *See* Vegetarian main courses.

Meatloaf

Homestyle Meatloaf, 178

Mediterranean Glazed Turkey Breast, 57

Mediterranean Stuffed Mushrooms, 164

Mediterranean Vegetables with Orzo, 103

Menus

Asian-flavored Dinner for 6, 147

Casual Appetizer Party for 6 to 8, 22

Casual Dinner for 4 to 6, 149

Celebration Dinner for 6, 24

Holiday Dinner for 10, 71

Meatless Dinner for 4, 181

Provençal Dinner for 6, 79

Weekend Brunch for 6, 132

Weeknight Dinner for 5 to 6, 144

Meringues

Bonnie Stern's Pavlova, 158

Mexican Pesto, 106

Miso

Fish Fillets with Miso Dressing, 42

Mom's Salmon Loaf, 36

Monster Potato Hamburger Buns, 136

Mozzarella

Eggplant with Mozzarella and Tomato Sauce, 88

Muffins

Apple Bran Muffins, 133

Cheddar Sage Muffins, 131

Cranberry Banana Muffins, 132

Mushrooms

Beer Mushroom Gravy, 63

Cornish Hens with Wild Rice and Mushrooms, 54

Homemade Pizza, 124

Mediterranean Stuffed Mushrooms, 164

Mushroom and Bacon Open-face Sandwich, 121

Mushroom, Spinach and Ham Crêpes, 117

Roasted Portobello Mushroom and Fennel Salad, 108

Zucchini with Mushroom Stuffing, 104

Mustards, 34

Nachos

Salsa Nachos, 29

Napoleons. *See* Desserts.

Nuts, toasting, 107

Roasted Pear Salad with Candied Pecans and Blue Cheese, 110

Oats

Oatmeal Apricot Scones, 130

Oatmeal Crisp Cookies, 142

Oatmeal Currant Scones, 130

Rise and Shine Granola, 114

Old-fashioned Macaroni and Cheese, 168

Olives

Eggplant Olive Tapenade, 27

Olives with Fennel and Orange, 93

One-Dish Suppers

Baked Spaghetti Carbonara, 85

Cabbage Roll Bake, 82

Chicken and Spinach Pie, 92

Chicken Pot Pie, 56

Chickpea and Vegetable Curry, 94

Deep-dish Tamale pie, 68

Eggplant with Mozzarella and Tomato Sauce, 88

Risotto with Sausages and Tomatoes, 83

Roasted Drumsticks and Vegetables, 48

Santa Fe Chicken Wraps, 86

Speedy Baked Beans, 87

Tortellini Casserole, 84

Tourtière, 90

Turkey Shepherd's Pie, 89

Onions

French Onion Soup Bruschetta, 23

Prosciutto Onion Quiche, 119

Open-face Apricot Tart, 162

Oranges

Olives with Fennel and Orange, 93

Orange Yogurt Cheese, 182

Ricotta Orange Crêpes, 117

Roast Chicken with Orange and Sage, 173

Orzo. *See* Pastas.

Oven French Toast with
  Caramelized Apples, 115
Oven Home Fries with Peameal
  Bacon, 120
Oven Thai Rice, 102

Pancakes. *See* Crêpes.
Parchment paper, 15
Parsnips
  Roasted Mixed Vegetables,
    102
  Squash and Parsnip Soup, 31
Pastas
  Baked Spaghetti Carbonara,
    85
  Mediterranean Vegetables with
    Orzo, 103
  Old-fashioned Macaroni and
    Cheese, 168
  Tortellini Casserole, 84
Pastry. *See* Phyllo, Pies, Puff
  pastry.
Pavlova
  Bonnie Stern's Pavlova, 158
Peach Upside-down Cake, 149
Peameal bacon
  Oven Home Fries with
    Peameal Bacon, 120
  Peameal Bacon Roast, 175
Peanut Sauce, 26
Pears, 111
  Cranberry Pear Relish, 47
  Roasted Pear Salad with
    Candied Pecans and Blue
    Cheese, 110
Pecans
  Roasted Pear Salad with
    Candied Pecans and Blue
    Cheese, 110
Peppers. *See also* Chipotles.
  Mediterranean Vegetables with
    Orzo, 103
  Rainbow Pepper Salad, 170
  Summer Peppers, 98
Pesto. *See also* Pistou.
  Camembert Pesto Phyllo
    Cups, 25
  Homemade Pizza, 124
  Warm Chèvre Salad with
    Mexican Pesto, 106
Phyllo
  Apple Cranberry Strudel,
    154
  Camembert Pesto Phyllo
    Cups, 25
  Chicken and Spinach Pie, 92
  Vegetable Strudel, 126

Pies
  Apple Pie with Cheddar
    Pastry, 156
  Open-face Apricot Tart, 162
  Pumpkin Praline Pie, 160
Pistou, 41
Pita croutons, 104
Pizza
  Homemade Pizza, 124
  Tomato Basil Pizzettes, 24
Polenta
  Herbed Flank Steak with
    Polenta, 64
Pork. *See also* Bacon, Ham,
  Prosciutto.
  Asian-flavored Meatballs, 70
  Crispy Butterflied Pork Chops
    with Creole Sauce, 74
  Danish Meat Patties, 67
  Glazed Spareribs, 76
  Risotto with Sausages and
    Tomatoes, 83
  Roast Pork Loin with Apples,
    72
  safe temperature for doneness,
    13
  Thai Pork Tenderloin, 176
  Tourtière, 90
Portobellos. *See* Mushrooms.
Pot pies. *See* One-Dish Suppers.
Potatoes
  baked, 23
  Baked Sweet Potatoes, 75
  Colcannon Bake, 97
  Monster Potato Hamburger
    Buns, 136
  Oven Home Fries with
    Peameal Bacon, 120
  Potato and Bean Caesar Salad,
    105
  Potato Bread, 137
  Roasted Mixed Vegetables,
    102
  Roasted Rosemary Potatoes,
    99
  Roasted Sweet Potatoes, 99
  Stuffed Baked Potatoes, 169
Poultry. *See* Chicken, Cornish
  hens, Turkey.
Praline, 160
Prosciutto
  Apricot Prosciutto Wraps, 22
  Prosciutto Onion Quiche, 119
Puddings. *See* Desserts.
Puff pastry
  Fontina and Grape Flatbread,
    109

Lemon and White Chocolate
  Napoleons, 152
Pumpkin Praline Pie, 160

Quesadillas
  Black Bean and Cheese
    Quesadillas, 28
  Chicken Satay Quesadillas, 26
  Ham and Cheese Quesadillas,
    28
Quiches
  Prosciutto Onion Quiche, 119
Quick Berry Jam, 137
Quick Spinach Salad, 43
Quick Tomatoes Provençal, 139
Quickbreads. *See also* Muffins.
  Apricot Caraway Soda Bread,
    179
  Blueberry Cinnamon Loaf,
    134
  Blueberry Lemon Drop
    Biscuits, 129
  Cheddar and Sun-dried
    Tomato Soda Bread, 179
  Chive Gruyère Biscuits, 128
  Citrus Tea Bread, 180
  Oatmeal Apricot Scones, 130
  Oatmeal Currant Scones, 130
  Raisin and Rosemary Soda
    Bread, 179
  Raspberry Lemon Drop
    Biscuits, 129
  Rosemary Cheddar Biscuits,
    128

Rainbow Pepper Salad, 170
Raisin and Rosemary Soda Bread,
  179
Raita, 174
Raspberries
  Quick Berry Jam, 137
  Raspberry Lemon Drop
    Biscuits, 129
  Raspberry Vinaigrette, 110
Red Pepper Sauce, 50
Red Snapper with Herbed Bread
  Crumbs and Tartar Sauce,
  38
Relishes. *See* Condiments.
Rhubarb
  Rhubarb Coffee Cake, 146
  Strawberry Rhubarb Crunch,
    151
Rib Eye Roast with Beer
  Mushroom Gravy, 63
Rice. *See also* Wild rice.
  Baked Rice Pudding, 183

Oven Thai Rice, 102
Risotto with Sausages and
        Tomatoes, 83
Stir-fried Rice, 175
Ricotta Orange Crêpes, 117
Rise and Shine Granola, 114
Risotto with Sausages and
        Tomatoes, 83
Roast Chicken with Orange and
        Sage, 173
Roast Pork Loin with Apples, 72
Roast Prime Rib of Beef, 62
Roast Turkey with Dried
        Cranberry Dressing, 58
Roasted Asparagus, 77
Roasted Cauliflower, 94
Roasted Cherry Tomatoes, 36
Roasted Drumsticks and
        Vegetables, 48
Roasted Flat Chicken, 46
Roasted Garlic Bread, 140
Roasted Mixed Vegetables, 102
Roasted Pear Salad with Candied
        Pecans and Blue Cheese,
        110
Roasted Portobello Mushroom
        and Fennel Salad, 108
Roasted Rack of Lamb, 77
Roasted Rosemary Potatoes, 99
Roasted Tomato and Garlic Soup,
        32
Rosemary
    Lemon Rosemary Shortbread,
        141
    Roasted Rosemary Potatoes,
        99
    Rosemary Cheddar Biscuits,
        128
    Rosemary Garlic Fougasse,
        138

Safety
    convection toaster ovens, 17-
        18
    food safety, 16-17
    safe temperatures for
        doneness, 13-14
Sage
    Cheddar Sage Muffins, 131
    Roast Chicken with Orange
        and Sage, 173
Salad dressings
    Balsamic Vinaigrette, 108
    Raspberry Vinaigrette, 110
Salads
    Cabbage and Apple Salad, 91
    Cucumber Salad, 35

Greek Salad in Kaiser Crouton
        Cups, 112
Potato and Bean Caesar Salad,
        105
Quick Spinach Salad, 43
Rainbow Pepper Salad, 170
Raita, 174
Roasted Eggplant Salad, 88
Roasted Pear Salad with
        Candied Pecans and Blue
        Cheese, 110
Roasted Portobello Mushroom
        and Fennel Salad, 108
Warm Chèvre Salad with
        Mexican Pesto, 106
Salmon. See also Fish.
    Asparagus, Chèvre and
        Smoked Salmon Frittata,
        118
    Baked Lemon Salmon with
        Mango Salsa, 171
    Hoisin Orange Salmon, 35
    Maple-glazed Salmon, 34
    Mom's Salmon Loaf, 36
Salsa Nachos, 29
Salsas
    Corn Salsa, 60
    Fresh Strawberry Salsa, 165
    Fresh Tomato Salsa, 86
    Mango Salsa, 171
Sandwiches. See also Bruschetta,
        Burgers, Quesadillas,
        Wraps.
    Crab Melts, 166
    Mushroom and Bacon Open-
        face Sandwich, 121
Santa Fe Chicken Wraps, 86
Santa Fe Tofu Wraps, 86
Satays
    Chicken Satay Quesadillas, 26
Sauces. See also Condiments,
        Gravies, Salad dressings,
        Salsas, Yogurt.
    Barbecue Sauce, 76
    Chocolate Bourbon Sauce,
        159
    Creole Sauce, 74
    Green Sauce, 177
    Mexican Pesto, 106
    Peanut Sauce, 26
    Red Pepper Sauce, 50
    Tartar Sauce, 38
    Tomato Sauce, 80
Sausages
    Risotto with Sausages and
        Tomatoes, 83
Savory Dip, 30

Savory Shortbread Bites, 21
Scones, 130
Seafood. See also Fish.
    Fish Cakes, 43
    Shrimp with Tomato and Feta,
        44
Seeds, toasting, 107
Shortbread
    Classic Shortbread, 141
    Lavender Shortbread, 141
    Lemon Rosemary Shortbread,
        141
    Savory Shortbread Bites, 21
Shrimp with Tomato and Feta, 44
Side dishes. See Appetizers,
        Condiments, Pastas, Rice,
        Salads, Vegetables.
Snacks. See Appetizers.
Soufflés
    Easy Cheese Soufflé, 122
Soups. See also Stocks.
    Roasted Tomato and Garlic
        Soup, 32
    Squash and Parsnip Soup, 31
Sour milk, 131
Southwestern Wings, 30
Soybean paste. See Miso.
Spaghetti. See Pastas.
Spareribs, 76
Speedy Baked Beans, 87
Spinach
    Chicken and Spinach Pie, 92
    Mushroom, Spinach and Ham
        Crêpes, 117
    Quick Spinach Salad, 43
    Spinach, Cheddar and Ham
        Frittata, 118
Spreads. See also Salsas.
    Apple Butter, 137
    Baked Brie, 165
    Eggplant Olive Tapenade, 27
Squares
    Chocolate Chunk Cookie
        Squares, 144
    Date Squares, 143
Squash
    Roasted Mixed Vegetables,
        102
    Squash and Parsnip Soup, 31
Standard ovens. See Convection
        cooking, converting
        recipes.
Starters. See Appetizers.
Steak. See Beef.
Stir-fried Rice, 175
Stocks
    Turkey Stock, 59

Strawberries
　Brie and Strawberry Crêpes,
　　116
　Fresh Strawberry Salsa, 165
　Strawberry Rhubarb Crunch,
　　151
Striploin Steak Roast with Green
　　Sauce, 177
Strudels. *See* Desserts.
Stuffed Baked Potatoes, 169
Stuffed Baked Tomatoes, 101
Stuffed Chicken Breasts with
　　Goat Cheese and Red
　　Pepper Sauce, 50
Stuffings, 13
　Dried Cranberry and Apricot
　　Dressing, 58
　Zucchini with Mushroom
　　Stuffing, 104
Summer Peppers, 98
Sun-dried tomatoes. *See*
　　Tomatoes.
Sweet potatoes
　Baked Sweet Potatoes, 75

Tandoori Chicken with Raita,
　　174
Tapenade, 27
Tartar Sauce, 38
Tarts. *See* Pies.
Thai Pork Tenderloin, 176
Thyme-scented Leg of Lamb with
　　Beans, 78
Tilapia Mexicana, 40
Toaster ovens. *See* Convection
　　toaster ovens.
Tofu
　Santa Fe Tofu Wraps, 86
　Tofu with Sesame Hoisin
　　Glaze, 123
Tomatoes
　Breaded Veal in Tomato
　　Sauce, 80
　Cheddar and Sun-dried
　　Tomato Soda Bread, 179
　Eggplant with Mozzarella and
　　Tomato Sauce, 88
　Fresh Tomato Salsa, 86
　Homemade Pizza, 124
　Mediterranean Vegetables with
　　Orzo, 103
　Quick Tomatoes Provençal,
　　139
　Risotto with Sausages and
　　Tomatoes, 83

Roasted Cherry Tomatoes, 36
Roasted Tomato and Garlic
　　Soup, 32
Shrimp with Tomato and Feta,
　　44
Stuffed Baked Tomatoes, 101
Tomato and Olive Bruschetta,
　　167
Tomato Basil Pizzettes, 24
Tortellini Casserole, 84
Tourtière, 90
Trail mix
　Airplane Snacks, 20
Turkey
　Cider-glazed Turkey Breast, 57
　Mediterranean Glazed Turkey
　　Breast, 57
　Roast Turkey with Dried
　　Cranberry Dressing, 58
　safe temperature for doneness,
　　13
　stuffing, 13
　Turkey Burgers with Corn
　　Salsa, 60
　Turkey Shepherd's Pie, 89
　Turkey Stock, 59
Turnip and Apple Mash, 100
Tzatziki, 52

Upside-down cakes. *See* Cakes.

Veal
　Asian-flavored Meatballs, 70
　Breaded Veal in Tomato
　　Sauce, 80
　Danish Meat Patties, 67
Vegetables. *See also* individual
　　vegetables, Rice, Salads,
　　Soups.
　Baked Beets, 73
　baked potatoes, 23
　Baked Sweet Potatoes, 75
　Bean Stew, 78
　Broccoli Cheddar Gratin, 96
　Chickpea and Vegetable
　　Curry, 94
　Colcannon Bake, 97
　Mediterranean Stuffed
　　Mushrooms, 164
　Mediterranean Vegetables with
　　Orzo, 103
　Olives with Fennel and
　　Orange, 93
　Quick Tomatoes Provençal,
　　139

Roasted Asparagus, 77
Roasted Cauliflower, 94
Roasted Drumsticks and
　　Vegetables, 48
Roasted Mixed Vegetables,
　　102
Roasted Rosemary Potatoes,
　　99
Roasted Sweet Potatoes, 99
Speedy Baked Beans, 87
Stuffed Baked Potatoes, 169
Stuffed Baked Tomatoes, 101
Summer Peppers, 98
Turnip and Apple Mash,
　　100
Vegetable Strudel, 126
Zucchini with Mushroom
　　Stuffing, 104
Vegetarian main courses. *See also*
　　Brunch dishes.
Bean Stew, 78
Chickpea and Vegetable
　　Curry, 94
Eggplant with Mozzarella and
　　Tomato Sauce, 88
Mediterranean Vegetables with
　　Orzo, 103
Old-fashioned Macaroni and
　　Cheese, 168
Speedy Baked Beans, 87
Tofu and Spinach Pie, 92
Tortellini Casserole, 84
Vegetable Strudel, 126
Vinaigrettes. *See* Salad dressings.

Warm Chèvre Salad with
　　Mexican Pesto, 106
White chocolate. *See* Chocolate.
Whole Wheat Grain Bread, 135
Wild rice, 55
Wraps, 86

Yeast, 139
Yeast breads. *See* Breads, Pizzas.
Yogurt
　Orange Yogurt Cheese, 182
　Raita, 174
　Tzatziki, 52
　Yogurt Cheese, 158

Zucchini
　Mediterranean Vegetables with
　　Orzo, 103
　Zucchini with Mushroom
　　Stuffing, 104